SHREWD BUSINESS TACTICS

Shrewd Business Tactics

A. T. Atienza

Writers Club Press

San Jose New York Lincoln Shanghai

Shrewd Business Tactics

Writers Club Press
an imprint of iUniverse, Inc.

For information address:
iUniverse, Inc.
5220 S. 16th St., Suite 200
Lincoln, NE 68512
www.iuniverse.com

Some of the anecdotes and topics mentioned in this book were provided by former co-workers, co-managers, supervisors and managers and do not intend to discredit or promote management styles or beliefs of any company, business owner, employee or manager. The author does not guarantee success in managing a business by following the principles mentioned in this book. This book was written to provide information only and to follow the literary principles that "knowledge is power" and "freedom of expression".

ISBN: 0-595-22723-6

Printed in the United States of America

This book is dedicated to my family, my relatives, my previous co-workers, my co-managers, and to all my superiors in the corporations that I have worked for. Most of all, I give my thanks to my Heavenly Father for blessing me with the talent to write this book.

Contents

INTRODUCTION

This book is about my 23-year professional work life experience under different Asian/Oriental companies in the Philippines. I have gathered all these anecdotes primarily from my own personal experiences, secondarily from my fellow workers, fellow managers and superiors.

This book does not deal on all kinds of Asian or Oriental management styles, as there are perhaps quite a number of them in existence. Although this book touches some aspects of Philippine, Chinese and Japanese management styles, it captures the basic essence of their management style, culture and practices. It also discusses some aspects of western or American management techniques as an influence in these Asian companies.

In each of the anecdotes and topics narrated in this book, you will find the unique management styles and the shrewd business tactics that these companies and businessmen employ which you will uncover as you read along. These styles and lessons in managing a business lie underneath the stories that I am going to narrate to you. You may find some of these management styles and shrewd business tactics somewhat amusing because of the difference in culture between the east and the west. Some business tactics may not be within your standard of ethics. You may either agree or disagree with some of them. But this is what is really happening in the actual business world as far as the Asian environment is concerned, more specifically in the Philippines setting.

Now, let us clarify some things. The word "shrewd" is defined in the Webster's Dictionary as "sharp in practical matters, having or showing keen practical sense, piercing, quick, discerning, perceptive, discriminating, and intelligent". As you can see, the descriptive words are positive. But what comes to mind to anybody who hears the word is the negative aspect of the word which probably may connote of "a person motivated by vicious, wanton, or mischievous purposes".

Using the positive side of the word, what we really need today are shrewd corporate managers and entrepreneurs in order that the business enterprise would survive and stay profitable in these very difficult economic times. With a lot of companies and businesses downsizing and declaring bankruptcies, the rules of the business game has changed. Being open-minded in terms of acquiring new knowledge based on the experiences of other companies and entrepreneurs will greatly help us improve the way we manage our business. Having this knowledge gives us an edge over those who are ignorant of its existence. You, the reader, are two steps ahead of the pack.

The intention of this book is to tell the stories and topics so that the reader can learn lessons from each one of them. I know that you can pick golden nuggets buried under each anecdote that you will find useful in your line of work or in running your business. The stories, anecdotes and events narrated in this book do not, in any way, intend to discredit nor promote any company or any individual's action or philosophy.

Some of the anecdotes in this book are presented somewhat like the case studies that you find in graduate school of business.

I was fortunate to be employed in three giant companies in the Philippines and from which the topics narrated in this book were based upon. The first big company I worked for was United Laboratories, Inc., (Unilab) the biggest pharmaceutical company and the market leader in the pharmaceutical market in the Philippines. It is competing against the big multinational drug companies, which are based in the United States, Europe and Japan. I had the privilege of working in the Human Resource Development Group, Management Services, Internal Audit, Financial Systems and Control, Management Engineering (I was assigned in the company's subsidiary company, Krieger-Dickmann confectionery), Market Research and Brand Management (I was assigned in the company's subsidiary company, Therapharma, Inc.) Unilab's program of assigning its employees to different work areas was the best program of all because one was able to get exposure in different fields. I became part of it and it became my greatest advantage and asset.

The second big company I worked for was Universal Robina Corporation (URC), a sister company of Consolidated Foods Corporation (CFC), one of the biggest food conglomerates in the Philippines competing against other giants like Republic Flour Mills (RFM) and San Miguel Corporation (SMC). I worked as a Brand Manager in the Brand Management Department of URC.

The third big company I worked for is Yamaha-Yupangco, a joint venture between Japan's giant music and electronic company, Yamaha, and the Philippines' biggest distributor of musical and electronic products, Yupangco. I was initially a manager for the Dealership Operations and after which I became a branch manager of a Branch Store Operations.

I also had a short stint working for Concepcion Industries, Inc., part of the RFM-Concepcion Group of Companies, one of the top 3 food conglomerates in the Philippines, in the earlier part of my career.

This book aims to present some aspects of the eastern or oriental style of management and the shrewd business tactics that they employ. This book also touches some aspects of beliefs being followed by some entrepreneurs in their line of business. I am not in any way propagating any kind of belief and I leave it to the readers' discretion, opinions and discernment. You will learn lessons in properly managing some areas of the company you are working for. You will also find success formulas in running your own business and how to avoid the mistakes that have taken place in the following stories that I am now going to share with you. Enjoy.

PART I

BEGINNINGS

My ambition in life, when I was in grade school and high school, was to be a commercial artist. I was very good in art and I became very popular in school because of this God-given talent. I became a school artist and won several awards in painting and poster design.

However, things changed when I was about to finally decide what I would take up in college. Although my father did not prevent me from pursuing a career in art, I can sense that he has some reservations. I remember him saying, when I was a kid, that I cannot make a decent living out of being a painter and that I may end up a "starving artist". That stuck in my mind although my father may or might not meant it to be that way.

My other alternative was to take up a course in business or commerce, which I feel is the fastest way to get a job after graduation. And since my father worked in an office, I subconsciously pictured myself working also in an office environment after graduating from college. We were not a well-to-do family so I became practical-minded and thought of the welfare of my parents far above my real ambition to be an artist. "Anyway, you can use your talents as a hobby while you are doing a "real" job", my father used to say. I followed the route that he wanted me to do and I did not end up as a starving artist but I ended up as a frustrated artist.

After graduating from college with a degree in Business Administration and accounting as my major course, I got my first job as a payables accountant for Concepcion Industries, Inc. (C.I.I.), a Philippine company that is licensed to manufacture and sell Carrier air conditioners, an American brand. I was assigned in C.I.I.'s subsidiary company,

Republic Service Corporation (RSC), a service center for their air conditioner product.

During my first job, most of my accounting work pertained primarily with repair services. Republic Service Corporation made money for repair work on Carrier air conditioners that have expired warranties. Who else can better repair Carrier air conditioners but our company? R.S.C. controlled the market for repair services and maintenance check ups. The holding company is owned and managed by the twin brothers Raul and Jose Concepcion. Raul Concepcion was in charge of Concepcion Industries, Inc. and Republic Service Corporation while Jose Concepcion was in charge of Republic Flour Mills and their other food and agribusiness ventures. Each brother manages separate enterprise but is under one holding company under their family name.

"FEAR MANAGEMENT"

During my stay in Concepcion Industries, I noticed the fear of my co-employees, my lady supervisor and the other managers every time Raul Concepcion makes his regular rounds of all the offices. Since I am just a new worker fresh from college, I found it appalling to see workers jitter at the sight of the owner. His presence, however, did not scare me since I am just new and do not know him personally. I have never encountered his wrath, if ever there was one, which probably everyone is afraid of. What I have heard was that this owner yells at his managers. He has thus created an atmosphere of fear within the organization. I have not seen him yell or raised hell during my brief stay in that company although I was always cautious every time I would go near his office to bring checks to be signed by the company treasurer, who is related to the brothers. I noticed that the key managers within the executive wing were either the owner's relatives or close friends.

There are several employees whom I observed were working with that company for many years inspite of the low salary. I just do not know whether they could not get a job outside or are just contented staying there. This management style of creating fear in the organization must be working for the owner because not only did he succeed in attaining his goals of having his workers do more productive work but that his organization spends less in salaries and wages.

This fear management style is similar to what is being practiced at Yamaha-Yupangco, a joint venture company between the Japanese musical instrument and electronics giant, Yamaha, and Yupangco, a Philippine distributor, which I will discuss in a later chapter.

LET YOUR SON'S FEET GET WET

In due time, Jose Concepcion, began exposing his eldest son, Joey Concepcion, in the operations of the company. Until finally, giving the reins of management by bestowing to him the title of chief executive officer at a very young age. Joey just graduated from a prestigious business school in the United States. The father just believed in his son's capability. Anyway, the father believed that he could always guide his son while he stays in the background.

Joey came in very strong when he got into the position. He believed in aggressive marketing and advertising as the most effective promotional tool. He immediately mobilized all their advertising agencies to come up with aggressive advertising campaigns for their food products. More so because they have to compete with the other two giant food companies, namely, Universal Robina Corporation (URC)-Consolidated Foods Corporation (CFC), a family corporation owned by the Gokongweis, and the market leader, San Miguel Corporation, majority of the stocks owned by the Sorianos of Spanish heritage.

EXAGGERATING LINE EXTENSION

Joey Concepcion's family corporation is the licensed processor and distributor of Swift food products, an American brand of processed meat, for the Philippine market. Swift is just one of the brands that the company is managing. Swift brand is a separate division of the Concepcion group of companies. That is how big the Swift brand is and how important it is for the Concepcion family. Swift is a major player in the fight for supremacy in the processed food market. The brand name is well known and has a high reputation for quality. Swift's popular products are corned beef, hotdogs, luncheon meats, dressed chicken and other processed meat products. Knowing the strength of the Swift brand, Joey Concepcion had to bank on it because he felt that using the name Swift ensures success in the market place.

He said that his secret of finding out what his competitors are doing is that he makes it a point to visit all the big supermarkets and move around inside and find out the new products that are coming out and observing the behavior of consumers who are buying groceries. He is a one-man market research. He sometimes leaves his post as the chief executive officer; change his formal attire and dresses casually to go around groceries and supermarkets. He says he is not an armchair manager who just sits in the glass tower. He goes where the action is and that is, the groceries, supermarkets, wet market and public markets where the consumers go.

So when a competitor, Century Canning Corporation, introduced their very successful ready-to-eat canned tuna with different flavors, Joey immediately did not lose time and out rightly came out with his own version…the Swift canned tuna.

When another company introduced the very successful ready-to-eat Chinese noodle soup with different flavors, Joey was never left behind by the bandwagon. He immediately came out with Swift ready-to-eat noodles. There were other food categories that he went into that I lost track of.

Now the brand name Swift has somehow lost its true identity and the consumers do not know whether Swift is a meat company or a company that makes canned tuna or noodles.

THE FASTEST WAY TO GROW

Joey Concepcion, young, ambitious, and aggressive bought Selecta ice cream to fight Magnolia ice cream of San Miguel Corporation and Presto Ice Cream of CFC. Then he bought a local soft drink company, Cosmos Bottling Company, to fight it off with Coke and Pepsi. Joey knew that with "Sarsi" root beer and "Sunta" orange, foremost soft drink brands of Cosmos Bottling Company, he can grab a significant market share dominated by Coke and Pepsi by capitalizing on the Filipino psyche of attaching the Cosmos brands to the Filipino values and traditions. He banked on Sarsi and Sunta as original Filipino brands and believed that more Filipino consumers will patronize them because the brands are part of the Filipino heritage. He came up with soft drink television ads depicting Filipino values and culture. The ads made a connection between Sarsi as a legacy of an original Filipino soft drink brand that has been in the market for decades.

The original owners of Cosmos Bottling Company never advertise their soft drinks. It never fought head-on with Pepsi and Coke. It, nevertheless, developed its own market niche in the low price segment. Sarsi and Sunta were looked upon as low class soft drinks because they are cheap and were never advertised. Joey changed the personality of the Cosmos brands through heavy advertising. Sarsi and Sunta are still sold below the prices of Coke and Pepsi.

Joey did the same advertising strategy with Selecta Ice cream because a Filipino entrepreneur founded this company. The original owners of Selecta never dreamt of expansion. Selecta was never advertised. They were already happy with their market share and were happy with their earnings.

The original owners of Selecta mentioned that they did not want any more headaches that go with expansion. They just want a simple operation and earnings that is just enough. The Concepcions made an offer to both Selecta and Cosmos that they cannot refuse. Joey expanded and improved the manufacturing facilities of both businesses and hired new professional managers to help him run these new acquisitions.

His father, Jose Concepcion, then went into government service by becoming the Secretary of Trade and Industry upon invitation by former Philippine President Corazon Aquino after ousting the dictator, Ferdinand Marcos. Jose Concepcion's appointment was a mere payment of gratitude by Corazon Aquino for helping oust the dictator during the People Power Revolution in 1986.

Having control of the Department of Trade and Industry and his son running their corporation, the Concepcion family felt that they are now ready to compete head-on with the giants of the industry.

THIS BUSINESS OF ICE CREAM

The ice cream market in the Philippines is a difficult market to enter. The market is dominated by Magnolia ice cream, a brand by San Miguel Corporation followed by Presto Ice Cream of CFC and thirdly by other small brands like Selecta and Sorbetero.

These brands of ice creams are traditionally sold in groceries and supermarkets. To expand their market, Magnolia initiated the concept of ice cream parlors or ice cream restaurants, which they put up and situated in plush shopping malls to create a classy ice cream parlor. Magnolia ice creams were served in platters and cobblers. And they came out with ice cream menus offering different designs, mixtures, toppings, fruits and other syrups. They called the ice cream restaurants the Magnolia Ice Cream House. Later on when the concept succeeded, they sold franchises to other entrepreneurs. Now you can see outlets of Magnolia Ice Cream Houses all over the country owned by franchise holders. To make the ice cream parlors more inviting, the parlors also offered hamburger sandwiches and other fast food meals to go with the ice cream.

Aside from the concept of ice cream parlors, Magnolia made a step further by making available the ice cream not only in groceries and supermarkets but through small retail stores or what is known as variety stores or convenience stores located in the remotest places.

They also invented the concept of home delivery by assigning a small time dealer in a small county or municipality by giving him free ice cream freezers stocked only with Magnolia Ice Cream and allowing him to make deliveries on the doorsteps of the customers' houses. All the customer has to do is call by phone to place an order and it will be delivered on his doorstep. Or the customer may want to pick it up himself from the house of the dealer.

San Miguel Corporation (SMC) owns Magnolia, SMC can muscle the dealers to stock only SMC products such as San Miguel Beer, which is the market leader in beer. If the dealer carries competitive brands of SMC, it will refuse to deliver their hot selling products to the dealer unless the dealer takes out the competitive products away from its shelves.

THE REAL GUERILLA TACTIC

In the mid 70's however, a new and unknown brand of ice cream suddenly came out of the market. The new brand of ice cream was named "Coney Island". Its logo and design were American in appearance. It gave an impression of an imported brand of ice cream. The Coney Island ice cream was actually made in Manila from formulation and ingredients from the United States.

A student of the Asian Institute of Management, a premier MBA school in Southeast Asia, was tasked to design the marketing plan for "Coney Island" and he made it as his term paper in his class in marketing.

What "Coney Island" did was NOT to put up an ice cream parlor inside the shopping mall because it would directly compete head-on with Magnolia. Coney Island put up a small retail outlet like a scooping station just outside the premises of the mall. The scooping station was designed to look upbeat and looked "American" with red, blue and white colors and a logo depicting a merry-go-round.

Magnolia was selling mostly local fruit flavored ice creams and other standard flavors. Coney Island came out with entirely different flavors, mostly American and European flavors and gave them foreign sounding names. The market responded favorably because they are new flavors and they taste differently. Filipinos, in general, prefer to buy imported goods since they are perceived to have better quality even though it may cost a little more. Coney Island did not serve the ice creams in platters as what Magnolia is doing in their ice cream houses. They instead serve them in different sizes of cones and the customer can mix-match the flavors. They called their outlets "scooping stations".

Another strategy that Coney Island did was to price the ice cream higher than Magnolia's to create an impression that it is a superior kind of ice cream.

During the opening of the scooping station, Coney Island gave out 50% price off coupons to all the students at the Asian Institute of Management. The school is just a stone's throw from the mall. Since the students were mostly taking up MBA, most of them did their case readings at the scooping stations. This created traffic and commotion in the scooping station. What Coney Island did was that customers have to exchange their cash for coupons first before they can be served with ice cream. This created two lines in the scooping stations.

There was one line for getting the coupons and one line for getting your ice cream. From afar, this created quite a commotion and the place looks so busy. People who were milling around the mall became curious of what the commotion is all about and they began going to the scooping station.

Meanwhile, the MBA students were also scattered all over the scooping station reading their cases and eating ice cream at the same time. For the next 6 months, the Magnolia ice cream house inside the mall was practically empty. Coney Island succeeded in creating noise and coming out with an entirely new kind of ice cream and a new kind of marketing strategy. And the funny thing is, a student designed the strategy.

After their success in the scooping stations, Coney Island subsequently decided to enter the groceries and supermarkets to expand their market. But they do not want to hit Magnolia head-on in this arena. They have to create a different strategy in the supermarket area. Magnolia is very strong in the half gallon and one gallon sizes. What Coney Island did was to come out with sizes entirely different from what Magnolia is offering. They came out with a "junior leaguer" size, which is not really a half-gallon but smaller. At the same time, they came out with a "big leaguer" size, which is not exactly like one gallon but a little bit smaller. The market conceived the new sizes as good for money value and this packaging size concept entirely differentiated Coney Island from Magnolia in the eyes of the consumer.

PART II

THE JAPANESE CONNECTION

The Yupangco family was the first and only business group to get the exclusive distributorship of Yamaha musical instruments in the Philippines long before Yamaha became a household name in musical instruments, electronics, motorcycles, and sports products. The Yupangco patriarch started selling these musical instruments by peddling them door-to-door. He would put a couple of organs in his truck and would demonstrate the organs by actually playing on them, which he did, house-to-house.

He concentrated on selling Yamaha musical instruments more particularly organs and pianos. Yamaha was not yet very popular during the 50's and 60's so Yupangco worked hard by promoting the product from scratch. His hard work doing house-to-house promotion paid off. Sales began to pick up and the brand became popular more so when he started putting up a retail store. Yupangco drew the attention of the management of Yamaha in Japan because of his dedication in making the distributorship of Yamaha a success in the Philippines. The brand continued to take off and Yamaha became the number one selling musical instruments in the Philippines.

The story is told that at the height of Yupangco's success and Yamaha's popularity, he was stricken with illness. It was at his deathbed that he gave his last instructions to his three sons on how to go about the family business. All his three sons were graduates of a prestigious and exclusive private school in Manila. Philip Yupangco was the eldest and it was to him that the elderly Yupangco gave the reins of the family business. Since the family business has expanded into other ventures, some of these companies were given to his brother, Robert, to handle the Yupangco private electronic labels. Rene Yupangco, the youngest, was tasked to manage the Yamaha School of Music and other minor business ventures.

Since Philip took hold of the major Yamaha product line and being the eldest, he was designated the president of the group of companies, while his other two brothers were designated vice presidents of their respective divisions.

Because Philip was tasked to handle a major part of the business during the early stage of his career right after college, he was somewhat pressured to handle such a magnitude of responsibility at a young age. He was pressured to make the family venture a continuing success. He was now the head of the family with a huge responsibility to take care right after his father's death. He was driven to extreme hard work and pressure. This self-imposed pressure on himself forced him to pressure also his managers in order for them to exert the same dedication he has for the family business. He was known to have very short temper and easily flares up during manager's meetings.

But what is his secret of success. He took much from the business strategy of his father. "There is no substitute for hard work" mentored his father. The mere fact that his father struggled in his early years with promoting Yamaha laid the groundwork for his children to take over the reins easily. Philip continued the legacy of his father and the business acumen that he inherited from him.

The following are just some of the tactics that Philip employed in managing the exclusive distributorship of a musical giant such as Yamaha, which was taught to him by his father and from which his father also learned from the Japanese.

LEARN HOW TO PLAY A MUSICAL INSTRUMENT

First, it is an acknowledged truth that to sell musical instruments, one has to know how to play the instrument. This was the backbone of the business…actual demonstration of the musical instrument. In fact, it is the secret of the business. There must be somebody who knows how to play and demonstrate its vast capabilities, the computerized mechanism, that creates the different sounds of an electronic musical instrument.

How can a customer appreciate the beauty of its sound and its other capabilities if you do not know how to demonstrate it? The prospective buyer must actually listen to the sound of the instrument. The demonstrator or the musician must not only know how to play but must also know how to sell and close the sale. Not only must the demonstrator know how to play but also create gimmicks or develop "showmanship". He must keep the prospective customer mesmerized by his performance. But in the end, he must be able to close the sale.

ALWAYS COME UP WITH NEW PRODUCTS

The Japanese are known for innovativeness. They always come out with new products. This is good for a business selling any kind of hardware.

That is why the Yamaha stores always attract customers because Yamaha always come out with new products, which entices old customers to change their old models with new and high tech products and for new customers to try the Yamaha products.

You do not want to go to a store that displays the same old item over and over again. You want something new every time you come in for a visit. The presence of new products every time you come in signifies that your company is innovative and progressive. It always makes the music scene dynamic and exciting every time.

STORE LAYOUT

Another business tactic is on how the stores are designed externally and internally. This is one aspect that is not left to amateurs. Philip sees every detail of the design of all the branch stores of Yamaha. All must project an image of impeccable elegance. Once you enter a Yamaha store, you get a feeling of high-class elegance. The best interior designs are done on every store. This is one aspect that creates a very positive image of the store and it builds the name Yamaha as a very classy, high quality product.

The arrangement of displays is another aspect of the total concept. The lighting is also one aspect that should not be overlooked. Correct lighting inside the store creates a feeling of ambience.

WHY A TRAINING SCHOOL IS IMPORTANT TO THE BUSINESS

Another secret to the success of the Yamaha business is the creation of the Yamaha School of Music. How can you create future market for musical instruments if you do not prepare the young students for the future purchase of Yamaha musical instruments? And the way to do that is to make available a learning institution to prepare the foundation for learning any musical instrument?

Almost all kinds of musical lessons are taught in the Yamaha School of Music. That is why the Yamaha School of Music is a separate business by itself. This company hires competent music teachers to teach different musical instruments for grade school students and adults. Students of the music school are potential buyers of the Yamaha musical instruments.

AGGRESSIVE ADVERTISING

Philip always believed in the power of advertising to help increase sales. During my stay with Yamaha, it gave me a solid belief in the power of advertising. When I was made branch manager of a Yamaha store, advertisement of our promotional campaigns help us to attain our sales goals. Philip Yupangco and his brothers are sincere believers in the power of advertisement. Philip always makes it a point that Yamaha should always be present in newspaper ads because these ads pull in the customers to our stores. Without these advertising supports, we would have to work double time just to attain our sales quotas every month. There would always be positive responses from prospective customers every time our main headquarters places ads in the papers. We would always have new customers coming in our doors every time an ad comes out. The power of these ads greatly influences the success of the company's biggest annual sale every month of October. This is our once-a-year biggest annual sale, which the company calls the "Handog Sale" (which means "gift" sale to the public), which I will expound later.

MONTHLY PROMO CAMPAIGN

Philip never runs out of ideas when it comes to sales promotional campaigns. He practically dictates to the Product Management Department what promotional campaigns to implement. He always does the initiative to come up with new promotional gimmicks every month. He never runs out of ideas. He is practically the big brand manager of the company.

For example, he would run a promo campaign for a particular digital organ with an offer of free lessons for the purchase of the organ. Next month, he would offer a buy-one-take one free item. All these promo campaigns always hit well with the public. All his offers are great deals and we always get significant increase in sales in our stores.

LIVE CONCERTS

Philip sees to it that we are booked for one whole year in terms of sponsoring promo events and concerts are concerned. These are musical concerts held at shopping malls, concert halls, and stage theatres.

Famous pianists, organists, and other well-known artists are billed during these concerts.

SCHOOL COMPETITIONS

Yamaha-Yupangco regularly conducts musical competitions among private exclusive schools. What we do is conduct internal competition within the school itself and the winners in each musical category are then entered into the area school competition after which a grand competition among the champion schools is held.

ANNUAL "HANDOG SALE"

The "Handog (a Filipino word meaning "gift") Sale is the biggest annual sale that Yamaha and Yupangco jointly undertake because this is where the biggest bulk of sales is generated. Most of the customers await this sale because sales prices are cut down in significant amounts. Transfer cost of the merchandise is lowered by Yamaha of Japan to make the annual sale a success. The "Handog Sale" is usually held in the month of October just in time before the start of the Christmas season, a good timing when people buy their early Christmas gifts. The annual sale runs for one whole week and a lot of fanfare goes with it.

Preparation for the "Handog Sale" is painstaking. From the planning stage like scouting for an exact location for the event up to the minute detail of the daily operations of the sale. One aspect of the preparation is the setting of the sales target for the annual sale. How many units of each particular model should we sell? These are then broken down by model, by product category, and by product segment.

Pricing is also critical. Prices are analyzed. Costing is analyzed. Expected margin is analyzed. How much percentage will we take out of the regular price? How much of each model do we need to stock before the grand sale? How many should we order from Yamaha in Japan? We consider the lead-time before these shipments arrived and we have to inform Yamaha ahead of time. Every detail has to be planned out a year before the sale is to happen. How are the sales quotas going to be broken down and be assigned to each branch store and to our dealers?

What kind of advertising campaigns should our advertising agencies prepare? We have to review the print ads. We have to review the design and total concept of the ads. What products are we going to include in the ads? How is the ad going to be presented? How many full-page ads are we going to put out? How many newspapers?

What usually happens is we choose the main venue of the sale like a coliseum or a well-known convention center. While we may have a coliseum as our main venue, the sale is simultaneously ongoing with our entire branch stores and dealers all over the country. All our company branch stores and dealers nationwide are synchronized with the annual sale. That is why anticipating the stocks needed to load the branch stores and the dealers is very important.

This "Handog Sale" or grand annual sale is a once-in-a-year event and it is meaningful to the customers because it only happens once a year. Unlike "Rooms-To-Go", a big furniture store in the U.S., which always advertises an "annual sale" or the "last sale of the year" almost every month, may create a credibility problem with the consumers. This is what Philip is concerned about. He does not want to offer this kind of sale every month; he wants the "Handog Sale" to be unique and true to its word, the best low price sale that happens only once a year.

TELEMARKETING

Another tool that is heavily imposed to all the branch stores is to do telemarketing. The head office requires a certain number of calls to be made to prospective customers every day. Each staff of the branch is given a minimum number of customers to call and make sales offers. Each staff, from the branch manager down to the sales associate, is given a minimum number of customers to call in a day and each are required to close the sale whenever possible. List of names to be called upon are taken from the guest book, which each branch store maintains. This is one of the most effective ways of promoting the products. Every branch store is required to maintain a guest book. Every customer that comes in the store has to be attended from the moment he walks through the door. We make the customer feel comfortable and to try to answer all his questions without pressure selling or "pushing". After presenting and demonstrating our products to the customer, we start closing the sale.

Every effort is done to close the sale, whenever possible, while the customer is inside the store. But if the customer is not ready, we ask him to sign our guest book and promise to send him upcoming product brochures and other promo materials to his address.

This list then becomes part of our prospective customer data bank, which is a very helpful tool when we do our telemarketing and direct mailers. These lists are qualified leads because these are prospective customers who came in the door signifying that they have an interest in the products. These same prospective customers, more often than not, purchase our products during any sale event. We make it a point to call on these prospective leads before any promotional sale take effect.

DIRECT MAILERS

We usually prepare one page promotional print material pertaining to an upcoming sales event and mail these in advance to our prospective customers listed in our guest book. These direct mailers are sent first before we do our telemarketing efforts. The direct mailers set the stage before we make our calls and it is easier to convince the prospective customer once they have read our advance mailers.

FLYERS

We give away flyers within the perimeters of the shopping mall. The flyer may either be a one-page ad of our ongoing promotional event or it may be in a form of a discount coupon either for the purchase of a product or for enrolment in one of our musical courses offered by our school of music. We hand this over to all people coming in and out of the shopping mall most especially to mothers tagging along their children since they are the best prospective customers for musical lessons.

MONTHLY SALES QUOTAS/TARGETS

This is Philip's forte when it comes to setting sales quotas per branch. He sees to it that every branch store attains its sales target. He pressures every branch manager to hit the monthly sales target. During the meeting, the branch managers and assistant managers are pounded and humiliated if they do not hit their quotas. Accolades are given to those who have attained their sales targets. It is not only the branch managers in charge of Yamaha product sales who are ridiculed during the meeting but also the school administrators in charge of the Yamaha School of Music.

If the monthly enrolment for a particular school of music is not attained, they are likewise humiliated. This humiliation is part of the scheme to put pressure on managers to hit their quotas. Some of those who cannot attain their successive monthly quotas are encouraged to resign.

Working in branch operations is one of the toughest jobs to have around. All areas of the company work on a sales quota system whether you work in brand management or dealer operations. This keeps the company always on the move. Pressure is exerted on all fronts. All managers, whether in sales or marketing or in finance, are all given pressures in their respective jobs. Only the brave and with guts survive in this company. Those who are weak and could not handle the pressure or those who think that the company is nuts quit after the first month of employment. Most, if not all, of the managers who cannot get a job elsewhere has to bear and grin living in this kind of management system. Almost all the managers, from the vice-president down to the supervisor, have acquired the characteristic traits and ruthlessness of the management style of Philip and his brothers. Although Robert and Rene do not exactly match to the style of their eldest brother, Philip probably thinks that this is the best way to attain success in this high wire game of selling.

COMMISSIONS AND INCENTIVES

Incentive schemes have always been an integral part of any sales effort. This is the motivation for the sales staff to hit their sales target. Philip knows the value of sales incentives and commissions. And sales people do strive with cash incentives. What can drive a sales person who only gets an average salary pay than cash sales incentive. Sales incentives vary in form. It usually is in the form of cash for selling more units of a product, which the company is trying to push or promote. Cash incentives light up any salesperson's face.

What is sometimes frustrating to the salesperson is that awarding of cash incentives takes a long time before it is received. The delay may be intentional on the part of the company in order to protect its cash flow or it may be due to several factors such as the time it takes to compute the incentives by one accountant. Or it may be that the delay is designed so as to spread the giving out of incentives to keep the sales staff on their toes. Giving it in bulk at one time may lead to laziness on the part of the sales staff because there is too much money to squander. So it is wise to always keep the sales force always expecting for something. The principle of dangling the reward on every salesman's noses is healthy for the company.

This reminds me of a story that my professor in political science told us during one of his classes in college. He narrated a very important lesson that the big landowners and big farm owners learned in managing their farms in the Visayan region of the Philippines. The farm managers, who usually are the landowners themselves, noticed that they always have a problem of absenteeism in their farm after every harvest when wages or bonuses are given to their farm workers. Every time the farm workers get a hefty sum of money after a good harvest or after getting a week's pay, the workers do not report for work the following Monday. What the farm manager learned was that the farm workers always celebrate their small fortune on drinking sprees on weekends. They celebrate as if it was their last days on earth. They party a lot and hypothetically paint the town red. The farm worker's wives, on the other hand, go to the big cities to go shopping. Some go on unofficial vacation. What happens is that there are no available farmhands to work in the farms.

Because of this revelation, the farm owners withheld a portion of these salaries and bonuses and intentionally delayed giving it to his workers. He followed the principle of "dangling the corn in a chicken's nose". He kept the workers always on tight cash situation to force them to work more hours for him. By making it tight, money wise, on the part of the workers, the owner can now control his workers to his own advantage.

INTERNAL COMPETITION

Another of Philip's scheme is to have the different units of the company compete with one another in terms of the attainment of their respective sales targets. He pampers the egos of his managers who perform well and embarrasses those who cannot attain their targets. It is during the manager's meetings that either he or his vice president presents the total sales performances of the different units of the company.

It is at this meeting that the managers may either be praised or humiliated.

YAMAHA WORLD ELECTONE COMPETITION

This is one of the most prestigious competitions of all. This competition was named after the Yamaha Electone electronic organ, which is Yamaha's top of the line product. It is so advanced and sophisticated that one organ player, playing the Electone, can sound like a full symphony orchestra with hundreds of musical instruments, sound effects and voices.

Competition is done on a multi-level basis. Competition starts from school level, to regional level, to national competitions and finally to the prestigious world competition in Japan. World champions in this competition are honored when they return to their native countries. National competitions are held in big convention centers to add prestige to the contest. It is a competition always awaited by serious musicians.

JOINT PROMO CAMPAIGN

Another marketing effort that proves to be effective is the joint promotional effort with restaurants. By combining the efforts of Yamaha and well-known fast food and other restaurants, both companies can co-promote their products to gain extra advertising mileage at less expense. One of our cooperative joint promo efforts is our presence in restaurants by providing organ or piano music inside their eateries while we at the same time give out Yamaha leaflets or flyers to the diners. Our regular joint promo effort is usually tied-in with McDonalds, Pizza Hut, and Jollibee restaurants. We get tremendous request for joint promo campaigns especially during Valentine's Day. We are requested to provide piano players as well as the musical instrument during this very important day. There is a stiff competition among restaurants during Valentine's Day to attract customers who go out on date. Our presence in these restaurants gives us the opportunity to show our products as well as demonstrate the astounding sounds of our musical instruments. The restaurant, on the other hand, gets the music for free and draws customers to dine in.

STORE DISPLAY

This is one aspect that is not left to chance. Every detail of the store's display is carefully studied and planned. From the concept of how the musical instruments are to be displayed and how it is to be laid out so that it is easy for the customers to walk around the store and make selections. This makes it easy also for our demonstrators to play on the instruments.

We see to it that all the products are already hooked up on electrical sockets so it is ready-to-demonstrate. Some of the smaller musical instruments are hooked on big and good quality amplifiers to project a clearer and better sound to attract the discriminating ear of the prospective customer.

One aspect of selling on the floor, which we learned from Philip, is that we should show and offer the high-ticket items first to the customer and then work down the product line if the customer shows resistance. The primary objective is to sell the customer the high-ticket item first. Selling the low price items first then selling up is not being smart. Philip sees to it that TV monitors, showing the latest music videos surround the store. The m.t.v.'s (music television) attract the attention of the customers as well as it provides music inside the store.

CUSTOMER SERVICE

Customer service is one aspect that is foremost in Yamaha's philosophy. Customer service is not just lip service. It is real customer service most especially in the branch store operations. All of our staff, from the branch manager down to the janitor, will do everything to provide excellent service to a customer.

When a customer purchases any of our products, we bring the product up to the parking lot and load the merchandise into the customer's vehicle. If we run out of electric adaptors, transformers or any accessory needed by the customer, we immediately purchase the items even from our competitors just to satisfy the customer and to complete the sale. If the customer cannot come to the store to purchase a certain item, we deliver the product right through their doorstep. If the customer brings in a product for repair to our store, we bring this product ourselves to our service center. We never allow the customer to be bothered by going to the service center. If the customer needs assistance in learning how to play the musical instrument and how to operate the functions of the instrument, we send our demonstrators to their homes and even conduct special lessons for the customer. We never say the word "NO" to the customer. We never say, "it cannot be done" to the customer.

Even if we have just closed the store for the day and have locked the doors, if a customer comes for a last minute purchase, we will happily open the doors again and let him in. Nobody in our sales staff goes home even though it will take awhile for the customer to make a last minute purchase. Any sale, whether big or small, is a sale for Yamaha.

If we do not have the model that the customer wants, we will search for it in other Yamaha stores and get it for the customer. That is why good relationships between branch managers count a lot in this strategy. A good branch manager should develop good relationships with other branch managers in order for them to work as a team in such situations as this. One should help one another in times of need especially when you need a particular product, which you do not have at the present time. If you do not have close relationships with the other branch managers, you will not gain their cooperation and it would be difficult for you to reach your sales quota for the month.

CLOSING A SALE

No one beats a Yamaha salesperson in closing a sale with a customer. It is an unwritten law that every customer that gets inside a Yamaha store should be able to make a purchase of any kind. Yamaha salespersons are creative, shrewd, and witty, in terms of closing any sale. That is how competitive and aggressive we are. We can outflank our major competitors on all fronts. We always outperform our major competitors such as National Panasonic and Casio. Yamaha has always been number one and has never been deposed of that position ever since.

DEALER MANAGEMENT

In order to control the market for musical and other electronic products in the market, Yupangco and company, the exclusive distributor of Yamaha in the Philippines, has built a network of independent dealers throughout the nation to run Yamaha school of Music and sell Yamaha products. These independent dealers compete not only with other music companies but also compete with Yupangco's own Yamaha store branches in their own territories. This is Philip's strategy of "survival of the fittest" between his own Yamaha branches and his dealers in order to flood the market with Yamaha products.

The selection of a dealer is very tedious and done very carefully. No one gets to be a Yamaha dealer outright. A prospective applicant for dealership must pass certain criteria to be qualified. The number one criterion is that the prospective applicant must have an inkling for music. The applicant himself must have some musical interest or any of his immediate family members.

Some of the existing dealers have at one time been a teacher in music or has a child who is a concert pianist or a champion in a Yamaha contest. It is not only the capital that is required to be qualified as an investor in a dealership, the owner of the dealership must have an interest in the field of music. This criterion has been proven to be a successful formula in operating a Yamaha dealership.

The same story is true with granting a franchise for McDonald's fast food. If the prospective applicant for a McDonald's franchise has no interest in food or has not even worked in a fast food chain, the applicant more often than not will fail in managing the fast food store. One must have a feel and love for the product before one can justify himself worthy to operate a business successfully. The capital required is a secondary requirement, but getting the right person is the primary consideration in awarding the franchise.

So if you want to hire somebody to manage your business, you must get somebody who has interest in your product and loves what he is doing.

PART III

MY STINT IN A GIANT PHARMACEUTICAL COMPANY

My employment with United Laboratories, Inc., one of the biggest drug companies in Southeast Asia and the market leader in the pharmaceutical market in the Philippines, was my most treasured one. First reason is the value they put on the human resource as the company's most important asset. Second reason is the valuable training I obtained from working at the different areas of the company. I was privileged to work in Human Resource Development Group, Management Engineering, Internal Audit, Financial Systems and Control, Market Research and Brand Management.

HUMBLE BEGINNINGS OF UNITED LABORATORIES

According to the stories of the old timers (pioneer employees) of United Laboratories, Inc., United Drug (the original name of United Laboratories, Inc.) started after World War 2. From the ashes of the war, Manila rose again to rebuild its commercial life. It was during this time that a Chinese-Filipino by the name of Jose Yao (who renamed himself Jose Y. Campos upon his naturalization) started a drugstore named United Drug in Santo Cristo Street in Binondo (part of Chinatown in busy Downtown Manila).

United Drug was primarily a retail drugstore, which became popular in that part of the city. Jose Campos or "J.Y." (As he was popularly known) went into this kind of business due to the encouragement of an American G.I. he befriended during the war. The story goes that this American G.I. had surplus military medicines which he did not have to bring back to the U.S. after the war and that he convinced Jose to put up a drugstore to make use of these surplus medicines. Since Jose did not know anything about drugs, he hired a licensed lady pharmacist to help him mixed drugs and sells them to the public. During this period, powders were mixed and made into tablets or syrups. Ready-made tablets and capsules were scarce after the war and the pharmacist has to mix powders at the back of the store, a makeshift laboratory. Jose and this American G.I. maintained their friendship and became business partners after the American went back to the States and continued shipping raw materials to Jose.

The retail drugstore business of United Drug continued to grow in the '50s. Thanks to the entrepreneurial spirit of Jose who was a hard-working entrepreneur. He practically runs the whole show by himself and he was very good in marketing. Jose never says "no" to a customer. When a customer comes to his drugstore to buy a certain medicine and it is not available in his store, Jose would tell the customer to wait for a few minutes while he prepares the medicine. In reality, he does not have the medicine on stock and what he would do is sneak back on his bicycle and hurriedly drive to one of his nearest competitor and buy that particular medicine. He would hurry back and give the medicine to the customer charging the same cost as he bought it from his competitor without adding any mark-up. That was just one way that Jose built his clientele. His motto is never say "no" or "we don't have it on stock". He believes that a good businessman must do everything he can to satisfy the customer. He would maintain a list of medicines frequently asked by his customers, which he does not presently carry, and sees to it that he has those products the next day. He has instructed all his counter salespersons to maintain a logbook and lists products that the customers always asked for and which they do not carry.

CHOOSING THE RIGHT BUSINESS PARTNER

As United Drug continued to grow, Jose realized that he is good in marketing but was not so good in financial matters. He then invited his bosom friend, Mariano K. Tan, to join him run United Drug as treasurer. Jose knows how strict Mariano is as regards money matters are concerned. Mariano was so strict that Jose cannot even make cash advances from the company coffers. Jose finally realized that their tandem would make a good team in managing United Drug. Jose was a natural salesman and tends to be lenient in terms of marketing expenses and in giving bonuses to employees while Mariano was strict in controlling the expenses of the new company. Their combination was a perfect match.

There is an Asian business principle that goes, "Do not choose your business partners just because they are your friends. The only reason why both of you are getting into business is to make profits. You are joining together because you do not have his qualities and he does not have your qualities. Do not get someone who is a clone of you. Get someone who can complement your weakness.

EXPANSION FOR GROWTH

When Jose finally settled down and had a family of his own, his brother-in -law, Howard Dee, tried to convince Jose to go into manufacturing of medicines. Jose was already contented with the success of his drugstore but Howard who has a very good foresight, convinced him otherwise. Howard was forward-looking and a visionary. Finally, Jose was persuaded to expand the company business by going into manufacturing. Jose and his partners acquired a property in Santa Mesa, a district in Manila, and began building the factory. Meanwhile, United Drug in Santo Cristo Street continued to do brisk retail business while the factory is being built.

J.Y. then executed the next secret of starting a business and that is "Get the best persons to help you manage your business". Since he did not know how to efficiently run a manufacturing firm, J.Y. began pirating brilliant people from the drug industry. He hired the topnotch in the medical board exam to head his research and development. He hired and pirated like mad. He hired brilliant pharmacists, chemists, engineers, accountants, and lawyers, marketing geniuses from competitors, production specialists, quality control experts, administrative managers from other business sectors.

In order to lend credibility to his products, he was able to get contract manufacturing jobs from leading American drug companies such as United American Pharmaceuticals and Westmont Pharmaceuticals. At the same time, he continued selling different brands of drugs at his retail outlet, those manufactured by Abbott, Merck, Bristol, Squibb, Parke-Davis, Pfizer and other giant pharmaceutical firms.

DESIGN A COMPANY THEME

J.Y. then started a different style of management. He called it the "paternalistic style of management". The "paternalistic style of management" is an Asian style of management wherein the owner of the company is looked upon as the "father" or "head of the family" of the company. All employees are treated like "family" or children of the "father". The company was run like a big "family". The" father" was respected and obeyed and his every decision was deemed to be for the betterment of the entire family.

J.Y. started using the "bayanihan spirit" (teambuilding) in all the mottos and creed of the company. He strongly believes that working, as a team is the secret of moving the company ahead. He saw to it that paintings depicting teambuilding be prominently displayed in all the lobbies of the company.

The painting typically depicts a number of people carrying a bamboo house being moved from one location to another. It signifies "working and helping one another". This depiction of people helping one another by carrying the house and having it moved to another place is the most effective way of conveying teamwork. J.Y. therefore instilled in the minds of every manager and employee about the significance of this theme.

THE IMPORTANCE OF SYSTEMS AND PROCEDURES

Unilab grew at lightning speed. However, it suffered the same fate as other small companies that started small and accelerated so fast...it fell behind the structuring and formalizing its systems and procedures. There were no written systems and procedures for each work area of the company. Every area basically started from scratch. There was no formal structure or organizational chart. Your area of responsibility and your boundaries are not well defined. Your relationship with the other departments is not well clarified. Your reporting functions above you and below you were not set up.

This is the situation in all the work areas of the company. The company, as a whole, runs on a system that was designed by the old traditional way.

And so it came to pass when two systems specialists from a reputable auditing and management firm came into the picture. Jesus Solomon and Sabas Isaguirre became the very first systems consultants assigned by Sycip, Gorres, Velayo and Associates, a well-known management consultancy firm, to put order into the system of Unilab. Top management of Unilab saw the value of the proposal from the consultancy firm and agreed to hire the two consultants. Jess and Sabas reviewed the prevailing system of every department of the company and made recommendations to improve and put order to everything. No stone was left unturned. It took a while before everything was put to order but the wait was worth it. Every one was required to follow the detailed manual of operations of their respective departments. Now everything was clear, smooth and orderly. Each worker and each manager knows exactly what is expected of him, his department and his role and contribution to the attainment of the company's overall objectives.

Why is this task very important? If you just let the present system prevail and do not improve on it, not only chaos and confusion will result, employees who have been doing their old system will reject the new system and behavioral problems will result. This is what happened with Ben and Jerry's Ice Cream in the U.S. Management was not able to professionally organize their system as early as possible and was already too late before they can remedy the problem. Employees have their own set of doing things and the human aspect of resistance to change came into play. Laying the foundation early, as regards formalizing and systematically organizing the system on every area, will prevent future disarray in functions and bring smooth operations to the company.

The days of trial and error are over. It is worth the investment of putting everything in order as early as possible before the present system becomes part of the culture of the organization, which later on may be hard to dismantle. It is also wise to get somebody from the outside to look inside the company and correct whatever is wrong with the present system. People inside see themselves as "perfect". People inside the organization tend to be myopic in vision. An outsider's view is more objective and they approach the problem on a professional level.

HOW TO EXPLOIT JOB DESCRIPTIONS

There was a time when our department, Personnel Department (before it was trendy to call it "Human Resource Department.") was tasked by top management to update the Job Descriptions for each and every job positions in the company. This task was being done to systematize the human resource management operations. They also want the employees to know what the demands of their jobs are and what are expected of them and whether they deliver the services based on what the job descriptions so describes.

The Senior Vice President for Administration, to whom we also report, asked each and every one of the department managers to review the job descriptions of their personnel. After which, our personnel director (now known as the human resource director) would call up all his friends, who are either human resource managers or directors of other pharmaceutical companies, and get a survey of their pay scale and their job descriptions. In this way, he can pick up some ideas of what is the prevailing pay rate outside of our organization and what particular job responsibilities they are presently doing that we may have over-looked.

What I find somewhat funny about the job descriptions for each job within the company is a small print appearing on the last part. The typical job description usually lists in numerical order the detailed description of the functions and responsibilities of a particular job position. Now maybe, in order for the company to protect itself from labor disputes or complaints from employees in the possible future, management inserted a "fine print" towards the end of the job descrip-tion. Guess what? The fine print states the following sentence "and to do other duties that may be assigned from time to time".

FABULOUS FRINGE BENEFITS

One of the biggest selling points of Unilab in hiring new employees is the fringe benefit that they offer. The fringe benefits are just fabulous.

We have free lunch everyday and even free meal when we do over-time work. We only pay a few cents to cover the cost of printing the meal ticket. The free meal has a strong psychological feeling of being united with everybody in the workforce. You all get the same kind of meal whether you are a supervisor or a subordinate. There is no discrimination as regards food is concerned.

We have vacation leave, sick leave, productivity incentive bonus, maternity and paternity leaves, wedding allowance (for those getting married), milk for dependents, free sack of rice every two months, bereavement aid (when a member of the family dies), hospitalization insurance, quarterly bonuses, Christmas bonus (also known as 13th month pay), profit sharing bonus, free sports facilities (the creation of a gym for employees to provide sports facilities such as basketball courts, swimming pool, pelota court, table tennis, chess, shower rooms, locker rooms).

In order to create a balance work atmosphere inside the company, sports tournaments are held all throughout the year. These are usually held after office hours. The most popular is the basketball competition among the different teams of the different divisions of the company (finance division versus marketing division, to name a few).

The productivity incentive bonus (P.I.B.) is given quarterly. However, as the name implies, it is based on productivity. Your particular job or position has a certain standard of output in which you have to achieve. You are rated on your attendance and your achievement of your targets for your particular job. The higher your score is for getting good attendance (meaning no tardiness, time off, absences) and getting high scores for attaining your goals in your job, the higher your productivity incentive bonus is.

Profit sharing is one of the best schemes the company has ever designed. It is given during the month of May every year because it is timed before the start of school, which comes in June. Employees usually set aside this windfall for expenses for the upcoming school term. The profit share to be distributed to all the employees is 10% of net income of the past year and is divided among all the employees. The computation of an employee's share depends also on the aggregate result of your productivity incentive bonus (PIB) for the past year. If your overall total rating is high for the productivity incentive bonus, you are sure to get a higher profit share.

In essence, management always sees to it that employees look forward for cash incentives all throughout the year. You expect productivity incentive bonus every quarter, a profit share during the middle of the year, and a Christmas bonus equivalent to one-month salary every December. That is why employees are always happy because the bonuses are spread out.

Another benefit that is oriented towards the families of employees is what they call the summer instruction program. During summer vacation when the employee's dependents are out of school, the company sponsors a summer instruction program. Different lessons in sports and crafts are offered to employee's dependents for free during the 2 summer months of April and May. Lessons offered are swimming, basketball, tennis, Hawaiian Tahitian dance, arts and crafts, and aerobic exercises

They also offer lessons for employees such as pelota game, archery, modern dance, chess, badminton, tennis, bodybuilding and aerobic exercises.

CHOOSING YOUR EMPLOYEES

Although there is an unwritten code regarding "selective" hiring, it is my hunch that hiring of employees is not entirely dependent on his qualifications but that he also should have a personal referral from someone already employed inside the company. This is especially true of very delicate positions in the company. The logic behind, in my opinion, is to assure that employees hired can be trusted because he or she has a debt of gratitude from whom he got his job recommendation. Therefore, it is assumed that he will not do any foolishness inside the company.

The establishment of a labor union inside the company is a big "no-no" in the minds of the owners. This is one reason that only referred applicants are considered for any kind of job in the company. I surmise that the company wants to hire only those who know somebody inside the company. This filters applicants who may have connections with any labor union. Management simply does not want a labor union organized inside the company, period. The owners have vowed that the company will never be penetrated by militant labor unions.

They believe that labor unions are divisive, that it has always been antagonistic to management, creates hostility between management and workers, and that it is disruptive to normal operations.

However, in order to lend credibility that labor is represented in all decisions affecting them and to impress everybody that there is democracy and a management's sensitivity to the needs of the workers, management created what they call an "Employees' Council" (E.C.), which is a quasi-labor union.

Employees elect the members of the Employees' Council. Each division of the company elects members as representatives to the E.C.

Part of the EC's major task is to formulate new programs to benefit the welfare of the employees and their families. The head of the EC is called the "chairman". The members of the council elect the chairman. Every program that the EC comes up has to be discussed by the body together with the members of top management. More often than not, management usually approves all the programs and projects of the EC. In fact, most of the ideas and benefit programs of the EC comes from management and all that EC has to do is pick it up from there.

Since most of the suggestions are for the benefit of the employees and their families, management, more often than not, approves the program and provides a budget for it.

MANAGEMENT BY OBJECTIVES

There was a time when "management by objectives" (MBO) became a fad in the business community. I remember the time when the whole company was obsessed with this new management thinking. Top management started this activity of defining what the corporate objective is. It was a series of meetings just to define the corporate objectives. The discussions were characterized by strong debates among the top executives.

Finally, after coming up with the "why we are in business and how do we get to achieve our objectives" philosophy, management then brought this concept down to the next level of corporate managers. The usual debate and meetings then took another series of months of discussions. After the different company divisions have defined their reason for existence, the MBO was then brought even further down to the level of department managers, then to the supervisory level and even down to the smallest unit of the company. Management believed that every unit of the company should know their own particular department's objective and contribution in relation to the achievement of the overall company's goal. It was a good idea of making everyone feel that each employee has a contribution, even though small, to the attainment of the company's grand objectives.

It sounded so funny when it was brought down to the smallest unit of the company. When the "general services department", which was also responsible for the janitorial services of the entire company, was asked its department objectives in relation to the company's overall objectives, they defined their department objective as "to provide janitorial services to all the company's facilities to the attainment of the corporate objective of providing quality medicines at affordable prices to as many patients in the Philippines and in Southeast Asia".

The long sessions and meetings took forever before every unit can have their objectives clearly written down because of the big size of the company. Volumes of paper work were filed from all working units of the company.

Now, these stacks of paperwork are now filed in archives to be opened in the future for posterity sake.

THE TRAINING PROGRAM THAT WENT WRONG

Training seminars are done in-house and seminar speakers are either managers inside the company or hired trainors from outside. If the seminar is about technical subjects of whom the company is not an expert, the company usually hire experts from the industry. Although it is cost-wise to just get somebody inside the company to do the training, employees prefer to listen to a speaker who comes from outside. They seem to be more credible from the point of view of the employees.

The 70's introduced into the corporate world a new trend in training programs, which involved motivational seminars copied from the concept of W. Clement Stones' Success Unlimited. It is basically patterned after motivational books of W. Clement Stones, Napoleon Hill, and Norman Vincent Peale. Og Mandino was one of the popular editors of Success Unlimited and a best selling author of motivational books.

The basic objective of these seminars is to motivate employees to give their best performance in their work and for them to have a positive mental attitude. These seminars hope to change employees' attitudes toward their work as well as their personal lives. It hopes to attain high employee moral, loyalty to the company, improve work performance, successful family life and the overall belief in oneself to be successful in whatever ambitions one has in life.

Rolly Quintos, a Filipino trainor, who got this technology from Success Systems in the United States, brought this so-called new concept of motivational training into the corporate world in the Philippines.

This new concept "clicked" in the corporate world and Unilab was one of the first companies to embrace and implement this into the human resource training program of the company.

The seminar called for a 5-whole day session for all employees, which was scheduled by department. It aims to train the rank and file positions of the company and the sessions are to be held at the company's auditorium. There were different sessions, which comprise the totality of the whole program, from lectures, meditation, and simulation exercises.

The whole program was seen as satisfactory because its purpose was to inject positive thinking and change people's work attitudes. There were sessions wherein participants were required to bring mats for them to lie down and meditate. The meditation sessions were like yoga exercises.

But one session that stood out as something unique and rather weird is a long session on "cursing". Rolly explained before we started doing the session that most of us, the seminar participants, have that inner hatred buried deep inside of us since our childhood. This inner hatred is serving as a stumbling block towards our attainment of our success in life. Some of these inner hatred stems from our experiences when we were abused as children and that some of us do hate either one of our parents.

We, the seminar participants, were then required to lie down on our mats, close our eyes, meditate, relax and do some concentration. Once we were relaxed, Rolly will begin cursing us. What he expects us to do is to curse back at him, squirm, shout back or express whatever emotions we wanted to unleash. This exercise, he said, would release the evil spirit of hatred living inside of us. The cursing took almost an hour but none of the participants, so I observed even though my eyes were closed, ever reacted to his cursing.

Little did we know that the shouting, yelling and cursing could be overhead outside of the walls of the auditorium. Unluckily, the Vice

Chairman of the Board, Mr. Howard Dee, was passing by the corridor and overheard the shouting inside the auditorium. Curiously, he opened the door of the auditorium and got the shock of his life when he actually saw the cursing being done on the employees. Mr. Dee, who is a devout Roman Catholic and a moralist, immediately ordered to stop the session. He condemned the training seminar as the most disgusting training program he has ever seen. Mr. Dee does not believe that cursing people is a good method of training people to be "successful". After that incident, we never heard of any succeeding session of the Success System and Motivational Seminar ever in our company.

HIRE A CONSULTANT TO CHANGE COMPANY POLICIES

How do you subtly change a company policy without being noticed?

There was a time when evaporated milk was being given to the employees' children at any age. These kids were being given several cans of milk every month as part of the company's fringe benefits for dependents. Children from infancy to about 12 years old were receiving milk rations. This was hailed as one of the most conscientious effort of management towards the welfare of the employee's dependents.

But one day, one of the medical doctors who is also an officer of the Employees Council, came out with a medical finding that milk is only beneficial for kids one year to 5 years old. He brought out several medical studies to back his pronouncements. Well, who could argue with a medical doctor? We surmised that his opinions are true to the letter. Guess what happened next? The Employees Council's benefit committee therefore cut the distribution of milk only to kids from one year old to five. Now compute the savings this has brought to the company. Did anyone contradict that finding nor did anyone protest the cutting down of milk rations? Nobody.

Another example. Seldom do Asian companies fire or layoff their employees even in bad economic conditions, which is in contrast with their western counterparts. It is inherent in Asian culture to keep its workers and together overcome the storm. It is only under very extreme cases wherein Asian companies lay off their employees. That is why there is what they call "lifetime employment" in Japan wherein "seniority" counts in terms of getting more privileges. Most Asian companies tend to protect their employees and their families.

How do you eliminate or reshuffle jobs that are no longer productive and at the same time avoid resistance from employees? Hire an outside consultant.

Our company hired a consultancy firm, which specializes in examining the productivity of certain job positions. They make recommendations on how the company can eliminate these jobs or transfer these workers in other areas wherein they can be more productive. This is similar to the "Pontius Pilate" principle of washing your hands of guilt and passing it to somebody else.

When the consultants initiated and finished the first part of the project, they subsequently trained selected teams of our own employees to take over. First on the list of the jobs to be examined are the general clerical positions. Each consultant worked with each and every individual general clerk to find out how they do their jobs. Part of the activity of examination is a time and motion study.

During the conduct of these evaluations, the employees were already having hints that their jobs may be in jeopardy. They already had a feeling that these whole exercise was just a disguise to eliminate their jobs or that they might be transferred somewhere else in the company.

Although the project took a year to finish because of the size of the company, the recommendations made by the outside consultants took a while before they were fully implemented by management. The transition was done slowly so as not to disrupt the morale of the work force. Management was cautious about the repercussions if drastic moves were undertaken right away. This typically illustrates the sensitivity of an Asian management system.

VALUE ANALYSIS / VALUE ENGINEERING

A new management concept came into United Laboratories, Inc. in the 70's brought in by a new set of industrial engineers hired by the company. It was called "value analysis and value engineering". No matter how technical the title might be or may sound, the bottom line is that its basic objective is to cut cost on all fronts. Period.

It is one of the most sensible management concepts ever developed. The results are tremendous. As far as cost reduction programs are concerned, it is my opinion that this concept is the best that was ever developed.

When the industrial engineers came into the company, they addressed the importance of this program more particularly to the manufacturing division where it would give the biggest impact in terms of cost reduction. The "VA-VE teams" as they called it, which is an acronym for "value analysis/value engineering", were scattered all over the company to look at every aspect of cost reduction on each of operation. But the initial concentration was zeroed-in on the aspect of cost of production more specifically on packaging materials for all the products of the company. And as you know, the company has thousands of products and product lines. And to cut down cost on one product alone would amount to significant savings for the company.

One very simple example of VA-VE operation is when they took a look at the packaging materials of one of the company's top selling brand of vitamin. They focused first on the individual box of the product and noticed that the box contains 5-color print on it. They suggested cutting the color print to 2. And did you know that the company saved millions of pesos just by having 2-color print?

The next item they looked at was the type of paper that was used for the individual box of this same vitamin product. The box was made of high-grade carton paper, which was quite expensive. The team then suggested to change the grade of paper to recycled type of carton paper. The company saved millions of pesos again just on this item alone.

Next they took a look at the label of the same product. The size of the label, the team said, is not proportionate to the size of the bottle. They then suggested shortening the size of the label just ¼ of half an inch of each side. They made some computations and voila the company again saved millions of pesos.

This is just one tiny bit of example of what the VA-VE team did to save millions of pesos for the company. They look at all the cost centers of the entire company and came out with tremendous recommendations that save millions upon millions of money for the company.

That is why I got the shock of my life when I went to San Francisco, California in 1997 when I accepted an invitation by an entrepreneur to view their manufacturing facilities and for me to consider joining their marketing group for his ice cream and a meat packing company. The owner of the company showed me all the manufacturing facilities of the ice cream plant and the meat processing plant. Afterwards, I was invited to attend an informal meeting with the manufacturing managers and their production staff. I was there as an observer to the meeting. The production manager discussed some of their problems in the manufacturing area.

The problems being discussed were varied. Some pertained to the quality problems of the product. Some pertained to the abnormal short shelf life of the meat product due to leakage problems in the plastic packaging. This resulted in spoilage and a high return of bad stocks by the dealers. Most, if not all, of the managers were either related or former classmates/buddies of the owner.

As I was listening during the meeting, I could sense that there is something wrong with the way the organization is being run by these managers in view of the many problems that are being laid down on the table during the meeting. It seems that incompetent managers, who do not know what they are doing, surround the owner and this is evident by the number of problems being discussed. How can this production manager be there in his position with so many problems in his hands and he does not even have a clue on how he is going to solve the problems.

What was happening was that he was throwing all the problems to the owner and he was just sitting there waiting for the solution to come out of the owner's mouth. What was so funny was that the owner was dictating to him what to do about each and every problem he has presented. The owner himself is not even a technical person.

What threw me out of my seat was when the production manager showed a sample of a packaged meat product in a supposed-to-be tight wrap plastic intended for freezing. I noticed that there was excess plastic on both sides of the packaged meat. There were at least 3 inches of excess plastic wrapper on both sides of the product. Those 3 inches of excess plastic on both ends is costing the company millions of dollars in waste without them knowing it. This is the kind of managers you do not want to manage your company. They may be your best buddies and they may be trustworthy. Or you may have owed them a debt of gratitude that is why you hired them. But hiring incompetent managers who do not have the experience and technical know-how will cause you to lose more money than you ever realize.

This is the criterion that he uses in hiring his accountants, advertising manager, sales managers and the rest of his employees. No wonder the company is not growing as fast as it should.

As I flew back to Florida, my mind was still thinking of the 3 inches of plastic in the frozen meat package and the millions of dollars running down the drain. I simply could not imagine it happening. These keen eyes that I have developed was due to my past experience of being exposed to the concept of value engineering. Without this experience, I wouldn't have noticed it either. I could have been the same production manager who could not see what needs to be seen. It really pays to hire experienced managers. Not only experienced managers but technically competent and professional ones. There is a saying that holds true;" you get what you pay for".

NEVER WOUND A KING

The sales growth of Unilab was phenomenal. But there is always this nagging problem that never stops. This was the problem of O.S. or Out-of-Stock finished goods. More often than not, there is always this O.S. problem especially with regard to the fast selling products. This also affected all the other subsidiary companies. Out-of-stock is also synonymous with L.S. or Lost Sales. The Manufacturing Division it seems cannot find a solution to this consistent problem.

Since this problem has gone unabated for quite so long, the Management Engineering department was tapped to investigate the problem. The procedure was to trace the movement of M.O. or Manufacturing Order document from the first department where it originates up to the finished good warehouse.

The M.O. document is triggered by the production-planning analyst of each subsidiary company from the time that the analyst sees an out-of-stock situation for a particular product appearing in the finished goods warehouse stock inventory report.

Since Unilab is such a big company, M.O.s passes through several departments such as raw material procurement, packaging materials procurement, and the production planning and scheduling department. Management Engineering has to investigate each and every department that the M.O. document passes through and find out the area that is causing the problem.

After months of investigation, Management Engineering came out with a surprise finding. It did not find anything wrong with the procedures of each and every department responsible for the smooth flow of the M.O.s. Each one of the departments was doing their job and was doing it well. The findings pointed the finger to just one culprit. It was found out that the only person creating all these chaos was the Vice President for Procurement and Logistics. This person happens to be a major stockholder and a trusted officer of the company.

Then why on earth is he the source of the problem? Based on the results of the study, it was found out that this vice president delay the approval or sometimes rejects the purchase of raw materials and other items.

My manager was really hot in presenting his unprecedented findings to the management committee to get the shock of their lives and to solve this problem once and for all. My manager says that he has enough evidence to present. Maybe my manager thinks that this would be his break to get recognized and get a promotion for this unusual discovery.

I was hesitant about his plan to expose the culprit. How could you nail a vice president who is also a major stockholder? I had my doubts but what can I do? He nevertheless presented his findings.

What I discovered later was that the vice president might have deliberately created this problem. He intentionally withheld approval for the procurement of raw materials and packaging materials. This causes the perennial out-of-stock situation. Now analyze the rationale behind this queer management style.

Well, review your knowledge about "just-in-time-production", "source the cheapest raw materials first", "adjust your selling prices after an out-of-stock situation" and other strategies. I was dumbfounded. Lesson for today, never wound a king.

CHARISMATIC PRESIDENT

Jose "JoeGat" Gatchalian was the best thing that ever happened to United Laboratories. He was the most charismatic president the company has ever had. He led the company to great heights during his administration.

He came into Unilab as a consultant from Sycip, Gorres and Velayo, an auditing and management consultancy firm. He impressed management with his talents that he was hired permanently to take over the marketing functions of the company. He became an instant celebrity among the salesmen, medical representatives, marketing managers, field operations managers because of his dynamism, brilliancy in marketing and his charismatic personality.

His personality radiated aggressiveness, youthfulness (the youngest ever to hold the position of president), and no-nonsense management style. He is a workaholic and a visionary. He does not believe in watches or clocks that is why he does not wear any wristwatch. He believes that wristwatches prevent one from doing more work because a watch psychologically limits your time. You can never see any wall clock in his office.

Top management (the owners) was very happy with the way JoeGat has been running the company. JoeGat charmed the most important area of the company, the field sales people. He is of the opinion that if you can control the field sales division, and then you are in control of 80% of the company because the marketing and sales group is the lifeblood of the organization. Not only was he popular among the marketing and sales group but also the rest of the employee population. He exudes a personality of confidence and trustworthiness. He means what he says and says what he means. That separates a leader from an ordinary one. He projects his concern to all employees and he means business when he says the "buck stops here".

There was a time when he was having a meeting with the sales force pertaining to the future expansion of the company in other business lines when one of the medical representatives attending the meeting made a suggestion pertaining to the company's plan of entering into the high end dermatology line. JoeGat was impressed and asked him what his background was. The fellow answered that his line is in dermatology. JoeGat told him that starting the next day he is to report to the task force for the dermatology project at a higher job position.

It was during JoeGat's administration that United Laboratories, Inc. (Unilab) grew leaps and bounds in the pharmaceutical arena. Unilab was the undisputed market leader in the pharmaceutical market. It was during this time that company celebrations, like parties and rallies for hitting the sales targets, were prevalent. It was the glory days. Management kept giving bonuses to employees. Commissions and sales incentives were given left and right. Everybody was happy. As long as we are hitting our sales targets, bonuses will never die. It seems that there was no way that JoeGat could make a mistake because everything he touches turn to gold.

VENTURING INTO THE UNKNOWN

No one can beat success. With his tremendous clout with top management, JoeGat now redirected the company to expand into other ventures. Now is the time to go into other fields. Since the company is presently in control of the pharmaceutical market, it is about time to try another ballgame.

JoeGat's instincts tell him to expand the operations of the company to other businesses. And expand he did. He drove the company to go into eel culture business by having a joint venture with a Japanese company named Showa. Since eel is a very expensive delicacy in Japan, Unilab and Showa formed United-Showa Inc. and they put up an eel culture facility in the uppermost part of northern Luzon islands, where eels where found to grow faster.

While United-Showa was undergoing initial business, JoeGat went into the candy and snack business by getting the franchise of Krieger Confectionery of U.S. to manufacture and sell the Krieger line of hard and soft candies.

Thereafter, he put up Dickman snacks brand to manufacture and sell corn-based snacks. Since Unilab did not have the technology or the expertise in snack foods, Unilab pirated managers, supervisors, technical staff from a leader in snack foods, non-other than John Gokongwei's company, CFC Jack and Jill Snacks. Later, JoeGat joined the candy and snack business into one company and called it the Krieger-Dickman Company and put his brother-in-law as the General Manager of both companies.

JoeGat's next project was to talk with ROC pharmaceuticals of France, a dermatology specialty company, to manufacture and sell ROC's dermatology line in the Philippines.

This project never materialized.

During this time, Unilab and G.D.Searle of U.S. joined together to manufacture and sell the Searle drug lines in the Philippines. Although an American expatriate independently managed Searle, the American country manager usually reports periodically through meetings with Unilab's top management. The joint venture with Searle was one of the most successful endeavors of Unilab.

Unilab also made a joint venture with I.C.I. (Imperial Chemicals Inc.) of England to manufacture and sell ICI drug lines in the Philippines. The joint venture made a good start in terms of capturing market share. However, the business relationship did not last long and ICI pulled out of the partnership due to ICI's disagreement with Unilab's practice of using ICI's name for Unilab's other private brands. This is one business relationship that turned sour.

JoeGat's expansion projects were very aggressive and he drove Unilab to go to other types of businesses. It seems that everything would turn out gold and that nothing could go wrong.

DECENTRALIZATION

It was during JoeGat's administration that Bernie Villegas, a noted economist and founder of Center For Research and Communication in Manila, became one of Unilab's consultants for corporate long-range planning. Bernie made "decentralization" the buzzword all over the management circles during the 70's.

The concept sounds logical. If the corporation has grown so huge and so complex, it therefore needs to decentralize its operations and each of the company's divisions should act as a separate company standing on its own two feet with certain autonomy. This concept somehow frees the head office of details so it can concentrate its efforts more on the company's future directions.

The logic behind decentralization is to make each unit a profit center and that it should be weaned from the mother company. Each subsidiary should function independently by having its own personnel department, accounting department, sales department, and purchasing department. It is like having your own mini kingdom.

However, this concept sounds too good to be true in paper.

Before the advent of "decentralization", Unilab was managed centrally since its birth. No proposal from any subsidiary gets started without the blessings of the home office. It has worked perfectly so far and that was how things were done the traditional way.

The owners, however, were skeptical about this concept of decentralization from the beginning. They felt uneasy to let loose on their control of the subsidiaries.

And so they did a "quasi decentralization"

THE DANGER OF DECENTRALIZATION

A great lesson learned here is what happened with the Krieger candy and Dickmann snack venture of Unilab.

It was during the administration of JoeGat that Unilab went into the confectionery (candy) and snack food business. As was mentioned earlier, Krieger Confectionery was established in order that Unilab can set its foot in the consumer market.

Unilab do not know anything about candy manufacturing and marketing. There is no doubt that it is an expert in pharmaceuticals, but it does not know anything about the candy business. Since it is a project of JoeGat, top management gave its blessing. JoeGat placed his brother-in-law, Louie Berrei, in control of this new venture. Krieger has a clout of its own having the full blessing of none other than the president himself. Krieger was sort of run independently.

THE CANDY BUSINESS

The candy business is somewhat like a "backyard" industry in the Philippines. Most of those running a candy business are small entrepreneurs who operate a small factory with very simple operation. Cost cutting is the name of the game in order to have low overhead costs so that you can sell your candies at very affordable price. Some small-time entrepreneurs make their candies literally at the back of their house that is why this industry is called "backyard". This is a business wherein you don't really make a lot of money because of the relatively small volume, low profit margin and stiff competition.

The name of the game is pricing. You cannot use expensive ingredients because it will drive your cost up and you cannot price your candies up because the prices of candies are somewhat fixed. Sidewalk vendors and small convenience stores are the primary outlet for candies. They are primarily bought by piece, this accounts for the relatively small volume of sales. Small factories in Malabon, a district in Manila, make most of the well-known local brands. Gokongwei's CFC Corporation and other bigger companies like Ricoa, Candyman and Serg's are some of the larger companies doing candy manufacturing and marketing.

Gokongwei's company, as well as the other medium-size candy manufacturers, does a simple operation. There is usually one factory supervisor or manager and the rest are factory workers that operate the candy factory. The candies are then passed on to trade distributors. This is supposed to be a no frills, no fuzz kind of operations.

KRIEGER-DICKMANN'S UNIQUE OPERATION

Now what kind of operation did Louie Berrei, the general manager, do for Krieger.

First, he may have unconsciously organized the Krieger Company like a pharmaceutical company. He created positions for an assistant general manager, a marketing manager, a sales manager, a production manager, a quality control manager, an accounting manager, office clerks, secretaries, a factory manager and factory workers. As you will notice, the management side is top heavy.

The administrative offices, where all his managers hold office, look so elegant that you would think you are inside another drug company. The factory and its manufacturing operation was state of the art compared to the factories of the backyard competitors. But what's the price do you have to pay for this? Very high overhead cost.

The next plan of activity was to go on full radio advertising followed by print ads. Aside from making the candies available to the traditional outlets like convenience or variety stores, Louie decided to have the candies packed in bags of 50's, 100's, 200's, 400's and make them available in shelves of groceries and supermarkets. It was supposed to be a brilliant idea. His purpose was to sell in bulk versus what his other competitors are doing.

But the problem is that the consumers are not used to buying candies in bulk, they are customarily used to buying candies by piece along sidewalk stalls and smaller variety/convenience stores. Placing them in supermarket shelves was a strategy that he thought would make them sell more.

The company designated Connel Bros., as their official distributor. Connel's responsibility was to place the product in all trade outlets. Everything looked fine as planned. Remember that Krieger was acting now on its own as if it was operating as a separate and distinct company. It is supposed to be a profit center based on the principle of decentralization.

The hard candies initially made good strides in sales in the traditional outlets (sidewalk and convenience stores) in its initial salvo. With this very promising outlook, management decided to buy machineries to make soft candies. The present factory site then made provisions to house the soft candy operations.

While Krieger was initially doing its operations, management then started with its new venture, the snack food operations. Dickman corn snacks factory operations was put up just beside the candy operations. Pre-production tests were done before the actual launching of the corn based snacks product. Taste test was conducted and it showed favorable results. Everything turned out well during the feasibility studies and pre production tests. Newly hired managers of Unilab who were fresh graduates of the Asian Institute of Management, the prestigious school of MBA, evaluated pre-production run.

The company was highly energized. It was excited because of the initial success of its two new hard candy flavors Orange Tweet and Lemon Tweet, management decided to come out immediately with new flavors. It decided to come out with new products while the iron is hot. Then came the smashing success of Strawberry Tweet. It introduced a new fad in hard candies. The formulation of the strawberry flavor resembled the flavor of a real strawberry. And whether it was designed by accident or not, the formulation left red colors on your tongue and lips. This red color on one's lips and tongue became an instant hit among children and teen-agers. Everywhere you go, you can see red lips and red tongue among children and teen-agers. Strawberry Tweet started a fad. Sales of Strawberry Tweet skyrocketed.

THE POWER OF RUMOR

There is an Asian saying that goes, "when a fruit tree is thick-full of fruits, people will throw rocks on it in order that the fruits may fall to the ground". In other words, if other people see you succeeding, others who are envious will try their best to pull you down. That's what happened with Strawberry Tweet. Krieger's competitors did not take this success just sitting down. In order to counteract this success, they scattered a rumor that the red ingredient in Strawberry Tweet is addictive and is bad for children. The rumor spread like wild fire and children were then told not to buy Strawberry Tweet because it has "addictive drugs" on it. Sales of Strawberry Tweet plummeted. Krieger did not know what to do. No matter how much they explain, the rumor just keep on getting worse. In a last ditch effort, Krieger launched a promotional campaign which they call "Visit our Factory" plant tour which are targeted to all elementary and high schools to come and visit the factory. After the plant tour, free snacks and candies are given to visitors. There were a few schools that did visit the plant but this was before the "addicting drug" rumors started. But during the duration of the rumor, nobody dared to go visit the plant thinking that the free candies to be given to school children might indeed be contaminated with "addictive drugs". Strawberry Tweet was slowly dying. Thanks to the very effective rumor mongering strategy done by the competitors. Nobody really knew who engineered this rumor. No one may ever know. This story proves the destructing power of rumors in marketing.

HIGH INVENTORY LEVEL

But Krieger's problems were not yet over. Krieger continued to introduce new flavors. The introduction of new flavors was so fast that the market could not even catch up. There were so many flavors that the new flavors were even cannibalizing the existing flavors that were making money. By now the newer flavors were eating into the shares of the older flavors. The company was not making strides because it has flooded the market with too many flavors. It has created multiple inventories of different flavors. The company's resources were tied to a large volume of inventory. Sales in supermarkets were still dismal. Consumers still did not buy those big bags with 200 pieces and 300 pieces in it. The ones that were selling were the 50s only. The bigger sizes were practically gathering dust on the shelves.

DO NOT ANTAGONIZE YOUR DISTRIBUTOR

Another factor, speculated by some employees, which contributed to Krieger's headache, involved a suspected retaliation from its distributor. There were gossips inside the company that the reason for Krieger's start of down fall was its mistake of selling its products by its own sales force to the outlets being serviced by its assigned distributor. Krieger was trying to increase its sales but was hurting the dealers and distributor in the process.

Another theory is that Krieger was deliberately overstocking the trade so they will look good to top management.

On the first theory, there was supposed to be a standing agreement that Krieger should not do any selling of its products other than its designated distributor. Being discreet about the knowledge of underground tactics of Krieger, Krieger's distributor, in retaliation, continued to pick up large volume of products from the Krieger finished goods warehouse on a round the clock basis. Krieger thought all the while that stocks were moving fast. Little did Louie Berrie know that what the distributor was actually doing was just dumping all the candies in their warehouse and was never being placed in the supermarkets.

The distributor continued stocking its warehouse until the huge warehouse was full of Krieger candies. Then they just let it sit there for several months until they expire. Once the candies are in bad condition, the distributors returned the candies gradually back to Krieger. Krieger did not realize that it was dying a slow death. It was already too late when the company finally realized that the cancer has spread all over the organization.

The Dickman snacks had the same fate. The quality of the product deteriorated because of poor packaging. The snacks spoiled easily because of inferior plastic containers. The product had a very short life span and the quality of the product did not match up with the prevailing competitive snack foods. The snack business was in jeopardy too. Another problem was that the main ingredient of the snack products, corn grits, could only be purchased from Universal Robina Corporation, the biggest corn grit producer in the country. URC is also the manufacturer and marketer of Jack and Jill corn snacks, the market leader in snack foods.

Unilab's top management allowed Krieger to stand on its own two feet but failed.

This is one classic example of a failed decentralization.

But why did upper management have second thoughts on full decentralization? You just cannot let your managers' act without any clearance from head office. The owner's belief is that one should still have a full control of what is going on in its subsidiaries no matter how small the endeavor might be. It is not that easy to let go and allow your managers to run your business. That is why the owners cannot let go of the financial control aspect. If you let loose on the financial control especially with regard to promo expense (such as entertainment expense) this will be abused by your own managers.

Entertainment expense (representation or p.r. expenses) is the most abused expense item in any company. Sales personnel including salesmen, medical representatives, sales supervisors, sales managers have abused this privilege. That is why management has to be very careful in giving out this privilege.

MONDAY MORNING SHOCK

Many people say that unusual things happen when you least expect it. That was what happened one fine Monday morning when Unilab employees were clocking-in to work. The whole Unilab workforce got the shock of their life when they found out that JoeGat had just resigned and left the company the day before.

Rumors started flying around. Did he resign or got fired? The mood of the day was like somebody died. Its leader suddenly disappeared. Everybody seemed demoralized by the turn of events. The questions that came up in everybody's mind were "What do we do now? Who is going to lead us?"

We have heard that during the past several hours since JoeGat resigned (Or fired?), top key officials were having round the clock crisis meeting about his "quitting". They were debating on who should immediately replace JoeGat. Who could possibly replace JoeGat? He was such a charismatic leader. Who could equal his personality and his drive for excellence? They could not find one.

But top management has to choose somebody to replace him now. The company can't wait. It's got to put somebody at the helm of the organization. JY immediately called an emergency meeting with all the employees. Everyone was in attendance. Everyone wanted to hear from the horse's mouth what the real score is and who is going to be the next president. The meeting place was tense. Everyone was apprehensive. What will happen with Unilab now?

JY finally took center stage and stood in front of the employees. Although he was trying to be discreet about JoeGat's resignation by telling everyone that they (upper management) cannot prevent JoeGat from pursuing other career, he is requesting that we all move forward from here and not let the gains and our growth go to waste. Although JY was trying to show strength in front of his employees, it is evident in his facial expression that something went wrong somewhere and he could not hide it. Thereafter, he called to the stage, our Vice President for Finance, Mike Gastrock, and announced that Mike is going to be our new president.

Mike started his career with the company as a bookkeeper way back during the United Drug (drugstore retail) days. He moved up the ladder, became a trusted accountant and held several managerial jobs in the Finance Division. He is humble and soft spoken. He is well liked by the employees in his division as well as respected by other employees. His low profile character and pleasant personality was the deciding factor, I think, for his selection as president to replace JoeGat. Mike may not be as brilliant and aggressive as JoeGat, but upper management felt that the company needed a man who the employees can look up as a "people" leader especially during these trying times. Maybe management was thinking that Mike could hold this position, as a transition president, until such time that they can find a replacement for him.

The wound inflicted by JoeGat's resignation finally healed after a few months and Unilab continued to be the market leader in the pharmaceutical market.

During the first few months of transition, nobody really knew what made JoeGat leave the company. However, one managing director speculated that the most probable reason JoeGat was asked to leave was due to the reason that he has put the whole company at risk. He has driven the company towards ventures wherein the company has no expertise on. His diversification program has placed the company in precarious situation. He spread the company's resources too thinly.

Others speculated that top management did not support his newer plans so JoeGat called it quits. Since he is a man of principles, he would rather quit than continue working without management support.

The last time we heard of JoeGat was that he moved to Universal Food Corporation, a catsup manufacturing company, as president.

PART IV

MY STINT IN MARKETING

I first got exposed in the field of marketing by getting a job as a staff analyst in Market Research. Little did I know, at that time, that a background in market research was the best entry point in marketing, aside from being a salesman. Because you are exposed to statistics and a ton of marketing data, you therefore develop a discipline of using hard facts to back up your marketing programs, which was valuable to me when I went into Brand Management.

THIS BUSINESS OF PRODUCING AND MARKETING MEDICINES

TYPES OF PHARMACEUTICAL COMPANIES

A "me-too"(a copycat) or a "compounding"(one who just mix chemicals) kind of pharmaceutical company does not really have an honest-to-goodness research and development program, wherein it budgets a certain amount of money for its scientists and chemists to discover new medicines to cure diseases. Discovery of a breakthrough drug usually belong to the bigger drug companies who have the financial as well as logistic resources to spend on research. It can gamble its investments on researching new drugs, which may either be a winner or a loser. It all depends on how the new drug will perform in terms of its efficacy as well as its acceptance from the medical profession.

A "me-too" company, which has no "real" research and development, usually looks at the total market for pharmaceuticals to pinpoint market entry opportunities. The total market for pharmaceuticals is basically composed of drugs participating in each particular disease. A particular disease is a major market segment broken into smaller sub segments. For example, Tylenol is an analgesic and an antipyretic drug and is a brand participating in the sub-segment market of analgesic/antipyretic. The analgesic/antipyretic sub-segment is under the Somatic major market segment.

On the other hand, Maalox is an anti-acid drug, which is under the category of the antacid sub-segment market. The antacid sub-segment market is under the Gastro Intestinal Tract major market segment.

Tylenol is not the only analgesic/antipyretic drug in the market. It is competing with a number of competitive brands being marketed by other drug companies. You should look into the sales performance, market share, and growth rate of Tylenol versus its other competitive brands. If for example, the total market for the analgesic/antipyretic is growing rapidly, then the "me-too" company may decide to aim for a share of the total sub-segment market's growth. If however, the market is not growing, then the "me-too" company has no recourse but to get its share from the market leader or from the other competing brands.

A "me-too" product may or may not succeed. But a good "number 2" has a better chance of succeeding. A "me-too" product is directly copying a market leader. A "good number 2" has found a use or feature that the market leader is not using. That is why coming up with an identical product similar to that of the market leader is quite difficult in terms of finding a unique product positioning. Extra effort is needed and you should research on the other uses of the product, which the market leader is not presently capitalizing.

In order for a research-based pharmaceutical company to grow, it has to continuously develop new products. An example would be the discovery of penicillin as an antibiotic. The discovery of penicillin is a new drug as well as a new product for the company that developed it. By putting a brand name to penicillin, the company distinguishes itself from other penicillin brands. The definition of "new" product for a research-based company simply means that an entirely new drug has been discovered, which is not yet available to the medical profession. On the other hand, a "new" product for a "me-too" company is just a copycat of an existing product, which the company may not yet made available to its clientele although there maybe a thousand brands of penicillin already available in the market. For example, if a "me-too" company has not yet introduced a penicillin-type of antibiotic and it decided to come out with its own brand of penicillin and named it "Cillin", this brand would be considered a new product as far as this company is concerned.

A research-based company knows how much capital is needed to invest in research and development. Not all pharmaceutical companies have the technical expertise to do research nor can afford to do research. Only a handful can undertake a real and honest-to-goodness technical research. These are the companies who dedicated themselves to the research of new drugs for the improvement of human health. Other companies who are not in real research are what we call "compounders". These are companies who just mixed powders and other chemical ingredients to produce tablets, syrups, capsules, injectables and other drug forms, put a brand name to it, promote and sell it to the market.

A research-based drug company not only relies on the introduction of newly discovered drugs to increase their market share and profitability but they also rely on the income generated by their existing drugs in the market. Why is the existing drugs' sales performance so important? Because the existing drugs generate the income that will provide the funds for the research of new drugs.

But in order for these drug companies to grow, they must develop new technological breakthroughs. A new discovery may either earn for the company billions of dollars or it may cost a company tremendous loss if the product does not become successful in the market in terms of efficacy and acceptance by the medical practitioners. More devastating is if the new drug causes toxic side effects as what happened with the drug Thalidomide that caused birth defects. The company that developed the drug was sued worldwide for damages. It is either you make it or break it.

One predicament of either a research-based company or a "me-too" company is whether to venture and take a risk into a new field or not. But in reality, both types of company have no other choice but to come up with new products. Why? If they don't come up with new products, their competitors will. In launching a new product, the aim should be to make the product successful. There is no other choice. If you are a research-based company, you have to come up with a breakthrough drug. If you are a me-too company, you have to look for distinctiveness about your "new" product, which will meet the needs of the doctor, and for which the originators of the product have not talked about in their promotional materials.

HOW ARE DRUGS CLASSIFIED

Business is built on loyal customers. In this instance, these are the prescribing doctors who have fallen in love with your company and its products. You must maintain that love; nourish it always because your business is dependent on it.

In most Asian countries, a prescribed drug that has been in the market for several decades ultimately becomes an "over-the-counter" (O.T.C.) drug (a drug you can just buy over-the-counter of a drugstore without the need for prescription). A particular drug becomes an O.T.C. product if the Food and Drug Administration no longer requires prescription for it. A drug can also be considered an O.T.C. product if more than 50% of its sales come from purchases in the drugstore without prescription. Since sale of pharmaceutical products are not very strict in some Asian countries, anybody can just walk in a drugstore and get the medicines that he wants even without prescription except for prohibitive or a narcotic type of drug.

Any type of business is built on loyal customers. The Pareto Law statement that 80% of your business comes from 20% of your customers still holds true. Stated in another manner, 20% of your loyal MD prescribers contribute 80% of your prescription sales. Giving these doctors your extra loving care will spell the difference between success and failure. Why should you waste your time in winning over the hardcore doctors who do not patronize your products and only prescribe competitive brands?

Another core product line that needs attention is the proprietary products or over-the-counter drugs because it is getting very expensive to launch "new" products into the market. Launching "new" products entails a substantial amount of capital and the chances of success are not guaranteed. If a pharmaceutical company wishes to grow faster, then it should consider marketing OTC products because it cannot depend solely on its ethical products (prescribed drugs) for company growth.

Take inventory of your products in the market. If more than 60% of your sales for a particular product are coming from OTC then it is an indication that you might want to consider going proprietary or mass media advertising rather than sticking it out in the very competitive prescription market. However, going proprietary marketing depends on the product you intend to market. Certain drugs or products are prohibited by the Food and Drug Administration to be advertised. Some prescription drugs may require revision in its formulation in order that they can be advertised or made available as OTC drug. Going mass marketing will increase the sales potential of the product especially if the product has built its reputation primarily as a prescription drug.

There is an advantage if a drug has established its reputation as a prescription drug. There is a big difference in the consumers' perception of trust between a drug launched immediately as a proprietary product compared with a drug that started as a prescription drug and afterwards was promoted in the mass media. Consumer perception on both products will entirely be different. The second type of product will have a better chance of being successful versus the drug launched immediately as a proprietary drug. This is similar to what happened when Vicks introduced an analgesic/cough and cold tablet named "Headway" which they launched directly to the mass media. This drug never started as a prescription drug. The product did not last long although a substantial amount of money was poured in for its advertising campaign. Compare this with "Neozep" cold tablet by Myra Pharmaceuticals, a subsidiary of United Lab. Neozep started as a prescription cold tablet and became a very popular anti cold drug among doctors and patients. When United Lab decided to promote this as a proprietary drug, it did not exert too much effort because there was already an acceptance among the consumers. With Unilab's substantial budget for advertising, Neozep took off like a rocket ship and became the market leader in the proprietary market for colds.

Unilab was not really new in the marketing of proprietary drugs. In the '50s, Unilab through its United American Pharmaceutical subsidiary launched its highly popular children's vitamin syrup with a brand name of United American "Tiki Tiki" (pronounced tee kee-tee kee). It was heavily advertised on radio (then the only popular communication medium before the advent of television). It was so popular that any kid or adult can sing the radio jingle. The radio ad was present in all radio programs especially "soap operas".

Most of the popular radio ads during that time were for analgesics (pain relievers) and for fever. Drugs like Bayer's "Aspirin", Sterling's "Cortal", "Cafeaspirina", "Alka Seltzer", "St. Joseph's Aspirin for Children" were also very popular because they are heard over the radio. Cold rub such as Vicks Vaporub, practically unchallenged and a market leader was also heavily advertised. Scott's Emulsion and Philip's Milk of Magnesia were advertised in newspapers and magazines. Other locally made over-the-counter drugs and herbal preparations were either advertised or spread by word of mouth.

It was only in the '80s that Unilab rethought its strategy of going all out in the proprietary market. As Unilab's marketing consultant, Eduardo Roberto, a professor of marketing in the Asian Institute of Management, recommended that Unilab go full blast in the proprietary market if it wants to grow.

Roberto said that it is getting more expensive and very competitive to launch ethical drugs into the market. Roberto said that it is easier to market O.T.C. drugs because it is easier to persuade the mass consumer market because you just have to play on the consumer's perception versus that of convincing a doctor about the merits of your product.

Unilab assigned one of its subsidiaries, Myra Pharmaceuticals, to take care of advertising efforts of all of Unilab's OTC products and its subsidiaries. As part of its expansion program, Myra Pharmaceuticals initially thought of coming out with an entirely new brand of analgesic to market by advertising it heavily similar to what Vick's did with its analgesic and cold tablet named "Headway". "Headway" was heavily advertised but it did not crack the market base of Unilab's "Neozep" cold tablet.

Myra then conducted its own market research to test market a totally new brand of analgesic. It was never launched. It stayed on the drawing board for several months. One of our physicians questioned the logic of launching a new brand of analgesic for the proprietary market. He said that it would take a long time for the consumers to be aware of the brand therefore it will take a big advertising budget to drum up awareness and interest of the public to buy this drug. What he suggested was that Unilab examine its currently prescribed analgesic drugs in the market and determine if it has a higher incidence of being bought over-the-counter versus it being prescribed. The report revealed that a Biomedis (a Unilab subsidiary) product named "Biogesic", an analgesic brand, was generating substantial sales coming from over-the-counter. Biogesic's advantage is that it has commanded a respect from its users because physicians prescribed it heavily. Biogesic started as a prescription drug therefore it had a built-in trust among the medical practitioners and patients themselves. It was the perfect drug to launch into the proprietary battlefield.

Biogesic was launched and heavily advertised. It is now one of the top selling proprietary drugs in the market today.

HOW TO DEMORALIZE YOUR SALES FORCE

Part of our function in the corporate marketing group was to present to the subsidiary marketing divisions an annual total pharmaceutical market study as part of an input to project the sales forecast for the coming year.

The first group that presented, during that annual marketing segment review was the Corporate Planning Group. They presented the economic outlook, price indices, GNPs and other statistics. They explained where the company has been, where it is now, where it intends to go, and how it intends to get there.

Thereafter, the different market segments of the pharmaceutical industry was presented, analyzed, scrutinized including expectations for the coming year.

Competitive analyses were also presented such as who are the major players and who are the leading market shareholders and losers.

There was an open forum in between the session, either to rebut the presentation or to augment and help make clarify issues.

Thereafter, our corporate marketing director would make a synthesis of the entire presentation. Based upon the study of the presenting groups, together with the Corporate Planning Department, it was determined that the pharmaceutical market will slow down in the coming year. Everybody who is presenting that very day unanimously agreed upon this finding. So in a nutshell, the marketing director was there to summarize the entire presentation and to tell everybody present that the prospects ahead are not so good because the industry is facing a slow down economy. He even gave concrete percentages on how much the market is going to decline.

Mr. Howard Dee, the vice chairman, came in during the last part of the conference to catch the remaining session. When the marketing director made his final analysis and synthesis, Mr. Howard Dee stood up and walked up the stage upon hearing the negative summary of the whole session.

The marketing director gave room for Mr. Dee as the vice-chairman grabbed the microphone and informed the whole participants that he does not believe that the total pharmaceutical industry would slow down and if there is a small chance it would, that it should not deter us, as a company, to grow in spite of the soothsayers' prediction. Mr. Dee said that if we want to succeed as a company, we could. Nobody can stop us from succeeding and attaining our goals to maintain our market leadership in the industry no matter what the economy is or what the economist may forecast for the coming year. He said that Unilab succeeded as a market leader because we believe that we are always strong and formidable.

Finally, after that contradictory statement from the vice-chairman and everybody has gone back to their work areas, the marketing director and the presenters were dumbfounded. The marketing director was still wondering why the vice chairman contradicted their statements? I asked myself, who is right? Is it Mr. Dee or is it presenters' group? The bottom line is…you don't say negative forecast or any of those doomsayers' predictions to your sales people…ever.

MULTI-DIVISIONAL STRATEGY

Another corporate strategy is internal competition.

How do you accomplish this?

Create subsidiaries, each having their own product lines and then have them compete in the marketplace against major competitors as well as with your fellow subsidiaries.

The strategy is to confuse the enemy and win. By creating different divisions, you make it hard for the existing competitors to compete and you at the same time discourage new entrants into the marketplace. Instead of losing your market share to your major competitors, it is better to lose it to one of your subsidiary companies.

However, the drawback here is that your own subsidiaries might be concentrated on beating their fellow counterparts and may lose sight of the real enemy, which are your major outside competitors.

Another drawback is self-cannibalization.

PENETRATION PRICING STRATEGY

As we mentioned earlier, a "me-too" company is one who produces and markets a product, which is similar to the market leader. The product is identical in terms of formulation and format. It is almost like a clone of the original product except for its name and presentation. The only differentiating factors that will distinguish a "me-too" product from the original are the "talking points" that the original product may not be saying. A "me-too" product may well be in a better position if it has found and exploited a benefit, which the market leader has not said about its product.

But for those of you who cannot say anything more from what the market leader is saying, then the "penetration pricing" strategy is highly recommended.

"Penetration pricing" strategy means that you enter the market by using pricing as your weapon. When I say pricing, I mean, getting into the marketplace by undercutting your major competitor's price by as much as 10%, 20%, 25% lower. The percentage difference depends on how wide your gross margin is. However, you can compensate a lower profit margin by the large volume of sales you will be generating because of your low price.

Penetration pricing strategy is the most effective way of getting fast into the marketplace and the fastest way to grab market share from your major competitor.

THE FALLACY OF THE PRODUCT LIFE CYCLE

The Central Marketing Group is a department within the corporate marketing group created by management as a "think tank" area to do marketing analysis and studies to aid management in decisions pertaining to long range planning.

One of the initial projects that it undertook was the Product Life Cycle Project. Its objective was to classify all of the products of the company according to where it is in the product life cycle.

The analysts who undertook the project were at that time students of marketing in the graduate school of business and the product life cycle is a hot subject in their marketing classes.

The basic logic of the concept of the product life cycle is that a product or brand goes through several stages in its life. The first stage is the introductory stage, then it goes to the second stage, which is the growth stage, thirdly the maturity stage, and finally to the decline stage.

After months of study, the group finally concluded that majority of the company's products were already in the maturity stage and that some are in the decline stage. The group's recommendation was either to launch new products to replace the matured products or to do "mercy killing" of the brands in the decline stage. They argued that these brands would subsequently die anyway. Why would the company keep them if they will just become a burden and drain the company's resources. Sounds logical.

When the group presented their findings to the management committee, one of those sitting in the panel was an operations manager from a subsidiary company. One of the products being recommended for "euthanasia" is a muscle relaxant, muscle pain reliever that was classified in the decline stage. However, this product is still pumping cash although it is already "matured". The operations manager voiced a strong disapproval for the recommendation of the group. He said that the product is selling well so why would the group recommend that the brand be eliminated. He does not see any logic to kill a brand that is doing well in sales although it may be in the maturity stage in the product life cycle.

Five years later, Unilab decided to go full blast in the proprietary drug market, this same brand that was recommended to be "killed" earlier was now reformulated to conform with the requirements of drugs being advertised and is now the top selling muscle pain reliever/ muscle relaxant oral preparation in the proprietary market. Talk about the product life cycle.

CORRUPTION IN PRODUCT SAMPLES

The marketing of pharmaceutical products is multi-faceted. A brand manager can use different marketing strategies and tactics. But the most popular among the promotional activities in this kind of business is the giving away of product samples to the MDs. The rationale behind the giving away of product samples is for the MDs to try the drug and test its efficacy among his patients. Product sampling is the most effective way of proving to the medical practitioner that your medicine really works. Product samples are also given to patients by the doctor as an initial start up dose while the patient waits for the filling of the rest of the prescription from the drugstore.

Physicians also give product samples to indigent patients who cannot afford to buy the medicines. Product samples are a sure way to make your doctor remember you and your product.

However, there are some unscrupulous doctors who sometimes abuse the product samples. Giving away samples has been the norm in promoting to the doctors by practically all of the drug companies; one has no choice but to join the bandwagon because everybody is doing it. But the practice has created a monster out of some physicians. Most of the bigger drug companies give generous quantity of product samples to physicians. So if you are just a small drug company and you are giving a miniscule quantity of samples, then some doctors may just ignore you and may not even remember your product or your company lest even prescribe your product.

But where do these excess product samples in the hands of the physician go? Because of the huge volume of product samples that physicians get from a lot of drug companies, whether big or small, a physician can literally put up a small warehouse for all the samples that he receives in a day. These samples are actually cash if you really think about it. Some corrupt doctors in the Asian environment sell these samples to an underground network that buys them and repacks them to be sold at a minimal price to smaller drugstores. So you will see that this abuse creates a new kind of competition. A pharmaceutical company competes with its own product samples that end up in the retail shelf of other smaller drugstores. These smaller drugstores are the one making a killing because of the large margin that they are earning.

THE LUCRATIVE BUSINESS OF PROHIBITIVE DRUGS

Hand in hand with the network of making money out of product samples are the sale of addictive drugs. This is another source of big bucks.

Did you know that big money is made out of selling cough syrups? There are a few "enterprising" but unscrupulous medical salesmen who are selling boxes and crates of cough syrups to drug addicts and to the drug syndicates. Taking an overdose of cough syrups gives the same effect as the other "drugs". It is the next best alternative to cocaine and a lot cheaper. Certain types of cold preparation and antihistamine are also being abused.

The latest discovery is the sniffing of a tube of "Rugby" bonding material which gives a "high" on drug addicts too. There certainly are new ways of getting "high" if opium, marijuana or injectables are not available.

PART V

WORKING IN BRAND MANAGEMENT

THE POWER BEHIND THE THRONE

During my first few months at Therapharma, Inc., a subsidiary of United Laboratories, Inc., I noticed that the overall sales performance of this company was below the sales targets even though the company had such wonderful products. Their products were considered classier and more geared towards the upper scale physicians. How come Therapharma was having a dismal sales performance?

I found out gradually that the field operations managers were not in good terms with the general manager. I had a hunch that the sales efforts of the field managers down to the medical representatives were manipulated to keep the performance below the standard.

I finally realized which particular group holds the power within the organization. The general manager became a lame duck. He could not enforce what he wants to do with his staff. His people would not cooperate. The poor sales performance of Therapharma kept reaching the home office. And soon, the corporate big wigs at the home office had to decide what action to take since Therapharma was continually making poor sales performance. They finally decided to transfer the general manager from Therapharma to the home office to be public relations manager. That is what you call a glorified demotion.

A new and young general manager by the name of Ven Mendoza, was installed. He was the former head of Unilab's generic company, UL Generics. Ven was easy to get along with. He knows how to handle people and was well liked by everybody. He has a full sense of humor and totally believes in the capacity and talents of his people. Ven befriended his sales operations managers. And he became their "buddy". Ven knows that his success will depend on the cooperation of the field operations group. His charisma and his good-natured character won the hearts of the field sales group. Therapharma slowly but surely was back on its way to the top.

During Ven's early days with the company, Therapharma was re-arming itself to fight aggressively into the cardiovascular market. It had old products like dipyridamole and some older forms of anti hypertensive drugs.

Unilab's corporate marketing board decided to strengthen the positioning of Therapharma in the cardiovascular market. This is in line with Therapharma's image of a high-class pharmaceutical company marketing only high-class lines of pharmaceutical products. Corporate management directed the new product development group to source new cardio products for Therapharma in line with the new thrust of the company. Management knew that the high-class image of Therapharma would blend well with the cardiovascular lines.

While Therapharma was on its way to the top of the charts with Ven's management and the employees regaining back their morale and enthusiasm due to Ven's effort, Unilab's top management decided to place Ven into other responsible position. He was abruptly promoted to country manager for the Indonesian operations of Unilab and he has to go there as soon as he can. Therapharma felt the loss of a well-admired leader. The promotions operations managers were questioning why top management has to send him away when Therapharma is doing so well. There were a lot of speculations about his being sent to Indonesia. Although it was a promotion, the first speculation was that Ven was not in good terms with the Vice President for Promotions who is very influential to the Senior Vice President of Marketing. And the only way to get rid of Ven is to put him someplace else.

Another theory was that another Division Manager; Enrique "Tito" Granda was being eyed to replace him at Therapharma. Tito was the former general manager of Biomedis. Tito had encountered "people problem" in Biomedis, he was eased out by management and was brought to the home office to be a manager "in exile". His fate was similar to what happened with Fernando Carbonell of Therapharma who also was eased out because of "people problem". But Tito's being in "exile" for 4 years was just temporary. His good friend and colleague since their medical representative days, Dr. Delfin Samson, a dentist by education, got promoted as President of Unilab after Mike Gastrock retired from the company. This was a good break for Tito. Dr. Samson, knowing the plight of Tito, assigned Tito to head Therapharma.

When Tito walked into Therapharma, he vowed that he is going to redeem back his glory and clear his name, which was tarnished during his Biomedis' days. He is going to prove to President Delfin Samson that the president did not make a mistake in choosing him to get back in to action.

Tito knew that he has to drastically change his management style. He practically dictated everything that everyone has to do and saw to it that all his decisions were followed to the letter. He implemented a totally different management style wherein he calls the shot every time.

He questioned every detail about the functions and programs of each department. He scrutinized all projects whether old or new from brand management, finance and administration, field sales operations, warehousing. No project or any activity will proceed without his blessing although these projects may have been approved by the previous administration. Tito knows that he will encounter resistance from the people upon his entry. He learned his lesson from Biomedis and this time he is not going to allow himself to be trampled again. Instead of being collared by the people, he did the reverse. He collared everybody. It was as if he declared "martial law" inside the company. He dictated everything that the company was supposed to undertake. He practically spoon-fed everybody on what to do and how the company is to run under his terms.

The staff knew that he has "connections" with the president and that they could not mess up with this guy. Tito revised everything about the marketing and more specifically the way the products are to be promoted to the doctors. His philosophy was that "this is my method and you should follow what I want, if my plans fail then I will be accountable to the president of Unilab, if my plans succeed you will reap the glory".

During the first year of his administration and with some luck, Therapharma having acquired very potential new cardiovascular products, Therapharma hit its sales target for the year exceeding expectations. As a reward for the employees' efforts, Tito gave generous incentives to everybody especially to the field sales force. One of his biggest prizes to everybody, literally everybody from janitor to managers, was a free trip to Hong Kong with shopping money, free food and accommodations during the 5-day vacation trip. Year after year, Therapharma consistently hit its sales targets and beat all the other subsidiary companies of Unilab. His sales incentives and prizes were easily approved because he can justify it through his outstanding sales performance. Tito has proven to everybody that he kept his words in terms of rewarding performance. From then on, the people supported him in all his plans, although they might not necessarily like his management style. But who cares as long as they take their vacation in Hong Kong every year.

HOW TO BECOME AN EFFECTIVE BRAND MANAGER

When I became Brandman (same as brand manager in other companies) for Therapharma, Inc. (a subsidiary company of Unilab), I noticed that the brand programs prepared by the brand men before me were primarily a list of promotional campaigns for a particular product. It was not an in-depth brand program. When I attended new product launchings before, the former brand man went on stage and just presented the promotional gimmicks that go with the product being launched. He was just on stage for about 10 to 15 minutes and that's it. There was no meat in the brand program. I felt that the audiences, which are the field sales people, were shortchanged. They were not provided with the total picture of the market. How can they appreciate their role in the war if they don't have a grasp of how the total battlefield looks like?

I totally changed the way brand programs were prepared. Since I came from Market Research, I injected solid marketing data into my brand program. This made my brand program more data based and backed up by concrete marketing information. My brand program was loaded with marketing statistics and market research data. I believe that a brand program can only be specific if I have solid and specific marketing data. Solid marketing data made me more confident of conceptualizing marketing strategies and tactics, which is the core of the brand program.

I also changed the way brand programs are to be presented to the field sales personnel. I used colorful graphics in my visual presentation and injected humor in all my slides. These help me make my presentation come alive. I do not want my presentation to be boring if I want to speak to them for more than an hour. I must hold their attention during my presentation therefore I must present fresh information, outstanding graphics, and I must be theatrical in the way I speak. I always inject humor in my visuals and in my oral presentation. I discovered that if you want your new product to be successful, you must win the confidence of the field sales force. That is the secret that I discovered during the first few months as a brand man. I befriended the sales supervisors, sales managers, and most specially the field salesmen/medical representatives.

I know that this strategy works because there was a time when the top brass of Therapharma and Unilab decided to launch two new products at the same time. I have some doubts about the success of such decision. How can you launch two products at the same time and expect the sales group to give their concentration to both of them. At the back of my mind, I know this will not work out.

We signified our reservations with the decision. Management said that it would be economical in terms of the cost of product launching since you have to conduct just one big product launch instead of two separate product rallies. No question about it. It would be more economical in terms of spending for product rallies. But I know deep in my mind that one of the new products will not be given concentration by our field force and would surely be sacrificed in lieu of the other product.

Turning a deaf ear to our argument, Therapharma still proceeded with the plan to launch two new products at the same time. One product, named Dicacin (pipemedic acid) is a drug found to be very effective against resistant urinary tract infection (u.t.i.). Another brand man was handling this brand. Dicacin was also found to be very effective against pseudomonas. In fact, the drug has many anti-infective properties. The "Pricing Czar" of Unilab who also is in charge of getting new patents from other companies and who was the prime mover for Dicacin, dictated to my co-brand man to position the brand not only as a urinary tract infection drug but also as an antibiotic, which is effective against pseudomonas. His suggestion that Dicacin implement a two-product positioning was confusing. We at Brand Department were even confused. I know from the start that Dicacin is a doomed product.

The other new product is a very promising cardiovascular drug. Luckily, this product was assigned to me. The brand name is Calcibloc (taken from the word calcium blocker), which was coined by the sales operation group and the brand management team. The drug is a new breakthrough for angina and hypertension. The market, in terms of monetary value, for cardiovascular drugs was very feasible. It is one of the most viable markets in the total pharmaceutical industry. How can you beat a market wherein there are as many people with cardiovascular diseases who take these medicines almost every day? This is a market wherein you just sit down and let the money to roll in.

The product launch dates of the two brands finally came. We toured practically every corner of the country to launch and conduct product rallies for the two brands to our field sales group. Each of the products was presented to the field operations group. This is a make or break presentation. At this level you can more or less determine if your product makes it or not depending on how your audience will respond to your presentation. I felt that this product rally was the ultimate test to determine which product could win the hearts of the field sales group. Which among the two will the field operations group support? We rallied our sales people to support both products but I know that the true picture will come out soon.

During the product launch or product rallies, the medical director and the medical manager presented the medical side of the products, thereafter, the general manager presented the overall objectives of the company, while the brand group presented the individual brand programs.

I was prepared. I had good visuals. I have rehearsed my oral presentation. I know I will make a good presentation because I was confident in my product and to myself as a presenter. I presented staggering statistics on how huge the market is for cardiovascular drugs most specifically for the calcium blockers. I felt that the game was over; my first slide was enough to convince the sales group that my product has a better potential. The rest of my presentation were icing on the cake. I presented all statistics available at my fingertips. I included our interviews with the top cardiologists of the country. I presented the reasons why the top cardiologists prefer a calcium blocker versus the other kinds of cardiovascular drugs against angina and hypertension. Before the end of my pitch, I illustrated how many prescriptions are written out by just one particular cardiologists and how many capsules or tablets each particular prescription contain and I magnified this by the number of patients the doctor sees a day. I learned this trick from our Pricing Czar and it was so effective that I rest my case after my presentation. I know that I have won the game. The succeeding slides just reinforced my earlier slides that this is the product that could help the field sales group attain their sales quotas.

If you are a medical rep or salesman, your primary concern is how do I make your life easier by achieving your sales quota and prescription quota at the earliest possible time and earn more commissions and sales incentives. Which do I choose, Dicacin, who has a weak and confusing product positioning and unattractive monetary incentive or Calcibloc, more feasible, clearly defined product and market positioning, more exciting market, and a more convincing presentation during the rally? One product has to be sacrificed in favor of another. Although the field operations group did not show it during the rally, I know one product has to die and one product has to live.

During the first week after the product rally, I knew I had a winner. One of the senior medical representatives came to me at the back of the convention center and confessed that the whole field operations group was behind my product and that they were very excited to go out into the field and start promoting Calcibloc.

The first few months were very exciting. We were already out of stock. We had to scramble to look for other raw material supplier; our present suppliers cannot cope with our orders. From then on, Calcibloc became a flag leader of Therapharma and the rest is history.

HOW TO ENSURE SUCCESS OF YOUR BRAND PROGRAM

In developing a brand program or marketing program, the brand manager responsible for the conceptualization of the program should check with the field sales group, who we will classify as the "tacticians", if his program is "doable" or implementable on the field level. A brand person should check his strategy development with the tacticians because there is a tactical requirement for each strategy. You cannot just design a program in the glass tower and hand over your program to the field sales people for implementation. That is not the way it works in the real world.

A strategy can have as many tactics. There are different roads toward reaching a destination. But the key secret in making a brand program or marketing program a success is if the strategist should sit down together with the tactician. The strategist should consult the tactician if the strategy he has conceptualized is implement able. Conversely, the tactician should consult the strategist if their course of action is aligned to the strategy of the company. They should both work as a team. If both parties do not talk to each other, the marketing programs will just be good in paper as what is happening to a lot of companies. It will be another marketing program so beautifully hard bound but is never implemented. The brand program is just placed in the marketing manager's bookshelf for posterity sake together with the other plans that never took off. If the strategist sees himself as a "know-all, snobbish, marketing guru" living by himself in the glass tower and just throws memorandums down to the field sales level, then he should not wonder why his marketing targets are not being met.

If you work for a me-too company, you must identify your product's distinctiveness that corresponds to an identified need of a doctor. You must "dress-up" your product, which refers to your product's "presentation". You must develop new "talking points" about your product, which again will have to be backed up by a verified need of a doctor.

And since your target market is the doctor, you must understand the doctors. You must understand the M.D. (medical doctor) market. What is an M.D. inside out? What are the M.D. demographics and psychographics? You must have a "best friend" knowledge of an M.D. For example, if you know a friend inside-out then your friend will be predictable. You will know how he will respond to different promo-

tional campaigns. You will anticipate how he thinks. You will anticipate how he will react to certain stimulus.

You should find out what his interest are. Does he like playing golf?
Is he a camera buff? Does he like watching basketball or baseball? Find
out his activities, interests and opinions.

In conceptualizing the marketing program, the planner should do
pilot testing. He should ask himself "what if?" questions. Questions
that will answer such problems as what can go wrong with the plan.
Questions such as "what if our major competitor responds to our price
cut?" "What if the government imposes restrictions on importation of
raw materials?" There is no time wasted for excessive planning.

HOW TO GET YOUR PROPOSALS APPROVED

If you are tasked with a project, do you want your proposals be
approved without any hitch? Of course. If you are tasked to make a
presentation to a management committee or a task force, do you want
your presentation to go smooth without any objection from the panel?

I learned the hard and long way but a field sales operations manager
taught me the secret of getting your proposals or your presentation go
smooth without anybody contradicting it. He advised me that during
the preparation of your project or proposal, consult every one that is
supposed to attend that particular meeting. Approach them for assistance in the conduct of your project and ask for their professional
opinion. They would be more than willing to give their professional
expertise. Most of all, approach the most ruthless member of the panel
for advice so he will side with you and not against you during the
actual meeting.

What the presenter or project leader erroneously does is that he does
not consult the other members of the panel or committee. This builds
ill feeling towards the manager tasked with heading the project. The
mistake that the project manager tends to make is to see himself as

more superior and knowledgeable than the rest of the pack and he never consults anybody. What happens next is that during his presentation, the rest of the panel will find fault in his proposals and kill it on the spot. But if you consulted them beforehand, they would surely cooperate with you. Do you think they will disagree with your presentation and downgrade your proposal? Of course not, because your proposal and presentation jives with what they have suggested. They certainly would not contradict themselves, would they?

THE QUESTION OF "DO YOU AIM FOR A SLICE OF AN EXISTING PIE?" OR "DO YOU AIM FOR POTENTIAL PIES?"

When I had a chance to talk with Dr. Vinzon Pineda, a well-known dermatologist in the Philippines and the owner/president of International Skin and Hair Corporation, he said that he is not in favor of pharmaceutical companies coming out with "me-too" products which are mostly over-the-counter drugs, low-priced, low profit margin, and highly imitated. He said that he carefully chooses his product and selects cosmetic or pharmaceutical lines, which are not heavily copied, are high priced, caters to the upper level income group, and has a high profit margin. He says that he does not want to waste his time on common products because he wants to project an image of a high-class-product-company. Dr. Pineda's dermatology practice caters mostly to the aristocrat segment of society because his professional services are expensive. He is well sought by celebrities and local movie stars for face-lift and other beauty regimen services.

He disagrees with the standard procedure of determining the sales forecast and market share being done by many companies. The standard procedure in determining sales forecast and targeting a particular market share for a particular product, moisturizer as an example, is by getting the total dollar amount (total market value) of all moisturizers in the marketplace, and target a certain percentage as the company's goal for its initial year of launch. Dr. Pineda argues that why should we limit ourselves to the existing pie or the present market size of moisturizers by getting a certain percentage out of the total. Dr. Pineda says that we should aim for a bigger forecast, bigger than what is reported, because it is his opinion that the market is not limited only to the total sales revenue of all companies combined, but there is far more potential than what we see in the actual records. He says as an example, if the total market for moisturizers (all sales generated by all companies selling moisturizer in a particular period) is ten million dollars, the standard procedure would be to determine how much sales do we aim out of the ten million dollars? We might peg a certain percentage of say 10% out of the 10 million. Dr. Pineda says that he will not aspire for 10% of the 10 million; he would rather aim for 20 million dollars because he feels that 10 million dollars is not the real potential market for moisturizers but it should be more than what the sellers are selling right now.

The question now is do you agree or disagree with Dr. Pineda's logic?"

PART VI

FINANCIAL MATTERS

THE HIGH COST OF "FLOATS"

When I was working in Financial Systems and Control, our primary task was to do troubleshooting projects for the Finance Division of the company. The different departments of the Finance Division approach our department to solve particular problems mainly involving systems and procedures or control measures. Thereafter, we make recommendations and propose improvements after doing an investigative study.

Also, part of the department's responsibility was to come up with incentive programs to improve the productivity of the employees of the division. We set aside a Job Recognition Program (JRP) which we hold every quarter to reward outstanding employees who excelled in the JRP. There are usually individual awards as well as group or departmental awards given during the ceremonies.

A part of our department is an extension office for a finance manager who was booted out of his department by his staff because of his very arrogant treatment of his employees. Management deemed it proper to just put him in a staff position and be a "think-tank" for the finance division, a work that never requires him to supervise or manage employees.

One day he called us into a meeting, to seek our assistance, because he says that he is conducting a very important study that he thinks will greatly save a lot of money for the company. He asks us to gather all documents coming from our depositary banks all over the country and get the deposit reports made by our field sales personnel, accountants, accounting managers, treasurers, cashiers in the different regions and anybody who has anything to do with money remittances.

The present system requires that finance managers, salesmen, cashiers, and everybody involved in remitting money to home office be coursed through the regional or out-of-town banks scattered all over the country.

This finance manager gave us a formula for computing the number of days from the time a cashier, in a remote area, deposits the company cash (comprising of collections in terms of cash, checks, money orders) to the regional bank and up to the time the head office of the bank credits us for such remittances. Initial results pointed delays in the remittance of money coming from the remote areas before they are fully credited to the company's account.

In a nutshell, the company is losing money in terms of interest, which the company should have earned if these deposits have been credited immediately to the company's account.

His formula gave us an idea of how much the company is losing, in monetary terms, because of the delay in the remittances of the different banks. The figures were staggering. Just by using simple interest formula, the company was being duped of the interest, which it should have earned. Thus the term "float" came into being. Money owned by the company being "floated" by the bank for the bank to earn their money.

The study was brilliant and we all applauded the finance manager. It was an eye opener. Who could have thought of such a brilliant idea? This guy is really a finance genius. His idea of "float" was something new to us during that time and even the vice president of finance was very well impressed.

That brilliant move stuck to my mind ever since and I continued to admire this finance manager even after 23 years has passed.

Then by accident, after 23 years, I stumbled upon an old book here in the United States of a very old issue of Financial Management published by the Harvard Business School. Lo and behold, there it is in one of the chapters was a discussion of…"floats".

BE VERY STRICT WHENEVER CASH GOES OUT OF YOUR POCKET

Part of my exposure in the Finance Division was being assigned in the Internal Audit Department of the company as an internal auditor. Being an internal auditor is a "prestigious" position in the company. It gave you "power" to "look into" certain things that needs reporting to top management. We were oriented towards the company doctrine that we were there to protect the interest of the company in all areas. We were looked upon as the "internal revenue" guys that everybody would try to avoid and not to mess up with.

What I noticed during my stay in this department is that all our audit reports not only goes to the vice president of finance but to one of the owners, Mr. Mariano K. Tan, the vice president for corporate funds/company treasurer/comptroller.

Final approval of all kinds of purchase requisitions passes through Mr. Tan's desk from a simple request of one box of paper clips up to the purchase of big machinery. Everything that has to do with the out-flow of company funds needs the signature of Mr. Tan. That is how strict the owners are with regard to company disbursements.

All purchase requisitions first need the approval of the department managers from which the request emanates.

Secondly, it requires the approval of the Budget and Cost depart-ment, to check whether the purchase conforms to the approved budget of the department. If the purchase is not according to the program and budget of the department, the request is denied. If a budget is pro-vided, then the request goes to the desk of Mr. Tan for final approval.

As regards cash reimbursements and cash advances are concerned, all these need the approval of Mr. Tan. The internal auditing department audits replenishments of petty cash and other expenses. Without the certification of the Internal Auditing Department, Mr. Tan will not approve any request. That is how he places high value in the internal audit endorsement.

The internal auditing department directly reports cash shortages incurred by salesmen to Mr. Tan. Discrepancies in stock handling by salesmen also go to Mr. Tan's desk. Practically everything that deals with company property custodianship and care passes through his desks.

All checks, whether for one box of pencil or for the payment of a million dollar equipment, needs his signature on the check. No check will be honored without the signature of Mr. Tan. Mr. Tan sets a day and time during the week just to sign voluminous quantity of checks. And his secretary is instructed that nobody bothers him in his office while he is signing all those checks. Mr. Tan signs each and every one of the checks. He does not use a signature machine like other company treasurer does. Not with Mr. Tan. He signs each one of them.

Our department audits everything, from salesman's cash handling and product stock handling. We conduct periodic stock inventory of the raw materials warehouse, finished goods warehouse, manufacturing supplies, engineering supplies, production output, manufacturing losses and discrepancies with manufacturing orders. We are the most powerful department in the entire company as regards protection of company interests are concerned.

The Chairman of the Board, Mr. Jose Y. Campos, however, sees the marketing division as the lifeblood of the company. He tends to lavish the marketing and sales division with cash and other incentives. He was once asked why he has a special treatment for people in marketing; he used an analogy for his answer. He says that "just like in any household, the member of the family who goes out to walk to sell products to make a living will certainly wear out his shoes compared with the other members of the household who just stay indoors. The soles of the shoes of the brother or sister who constantly walks to make a sale will surely wear out. The father therefore must always provide new shoes for the one doing a much harder work."

"RED FLAG" FOR AN AUDIT

Having been an internal auditor taught me several lessons in how to effectively conduct your investigative work. There are certain clues as to who, among our salesmen, cashiers, managers or anybody who is in custodian of cash or collections from customers, should we give special attention when it comes to audit. There is a "red flag" if it is found out from reliable sources, "spies" within the organization, that a particular employee or manager is involved in heavy drinking, womanizing, partying, drugs, gambling, or other vices. These employees or managers who are in charge of company funds are probable "embezzlers" or potential candidates for "fraudulent activities". It is therefore very important to have "eyes and ears" scattered within your organization to monitor the activities of employees handling delicate resources of the company. There is a big disadvantage for being too loose in terms of control measures because these employees are potential "time bombs" within your company. Managers or employees who are heavily indulged in vices will one day misuse company funds because they may not be able to control their "cravings".

ALWAYS PUT A TRUSTED FINANCE MANAGER IN A SUBSIDIARY COMPANY

This principle is very important especially for an Asian-run company. Always put your trusted finance manager in a subsidiary or a spun-off company. He should be placed there as the "eyes" and "ears" of the head office.

You may have a trusted general manager to run your subsidiary company but always place a finance guy to protect your cash, budget and other company property. The finance manager is your check and balance in that division or subsidiary. The general manager will have to display his proficiency in marketing and sales but do not leave to him the responsibility of cash and other assets. This is how Unilab works to counter balance the tendency of marketing to overspend and abuse its domain. It is preferable if you place a finance manager who is a former internal auditor so he knows the in's and out's of anomalies that may be encountered. As a saying goes, "a good cop can smell a rotten fish 50 miles away". His good sense of smell has been developed through passed experiences in auditing different areas of the company.

PART VII

SECRETS OF THE CHINESE STYLE OF DOING BUSINESS

When I started working as a Brand Manager for Universal Robina Corporation, one of the companies owned by John Gokongwei and managed by his brother Johnson Go, I was amazed at how these brothers run the company. I noticed that most of the managers are related to them in someway. Understandably, they have to trust the person that holds these delicate positions in the company. I was hired because my group product manager offered me the job. My group manager got hired because his sister's best friend has "connections" inside the company. So you see, you don't get hired just because you've got a college degree or experience. You've got to have connections inside.

I also discovered that my former girl classmate in high school was holding one of the highest positions in the company. She is the corporate comptroller and highly trusted by the owners. She mentioned to me that her father was a former tax consultant of the owner and upon his retirement recommended her to be an accountant with the company. She rose from a position of an accountant to a comptroller. Practically, all of the managers there did not become as they are. They have some connections somewhere. Trust is the word that best describes the quality of being hired as a manager. No amount of degrees can land you a job unless you know somebody. This is a sad fact of life. You may send a thousand resumes to the big companies but sad to say, they will just be thrown in the garbage no matter if you have a doctorate or a graduate degree. It just pays to know somebody inside. Some people are just lucky. Being there at the right time and right place. Sometimes it is just luck that spells the name of the game. You may never know when your luck may come or it may never come. But others believe that you can create your own luck if you work hard for it and show others of your drive and dedication.

I also fell victim to this method of sending executive resumes to as many of the big companies. I keep sending my resumes every week based upon the vacant positions appearing in the Sunday Classified Ads. Little did I realize that what I am doing is an exercise in futility.

LOW PRICE, HIGH VOLUME STRATEGY

Compared with other entrepreneurs, the Chinese have been known for their low price strategy. If you visit a very well known place called Divisoria, a commercial district in Manila, which is almost considered Chinatown, you will find the best bargains you could ever find. This is what they call the "Mecca" for great bargains. Most retailers go to this place to buy their merchandise for resale. Why? You get your merchandise at low prices, which mean that you can resell them also at lower prices.

Most of the Chinese businessmen do not have this usual business mentality of making an "instant killing". Some businessmen of other nationalities want to get their money back and earn as much profits at the earliest possible time. They simply want to get a hefty amount of money back fast. The primary objective of stockholders of big corporations in the western setting is to get their dividends as early as possible. Not the Chinese businessmen. Compared with the western businessmen, they are more patient. They would expand their business gradually. They would sell items at very low prices because they know that they could sell more in terms of volume. The lower your price is, the more you earn in terms of greater volume. Low price ultimately results in more volume of sales. This is a proven principle. People buy products because it is affordable. More consumers purchase goods that are priced low. Consumers want a bargain every time and they always compare prices. If a similar product is sold in two stores, the store that sells it lower usually gets the sale. That is just how the mind of a consumer works.

It does not have to be proven otherwise. People want bargains. That is why the Chinese sell by volume. The more you buy, the more discount you get. They sell items by the dozen even though they will only profit for nickels and dimes. Nickels and dimes multiplied by the bigger volume will generate more money. The name of the game as the Chinese say is, the faster the turnover of your merchandise is, and the faster the cash inflow is.

They do not want merchandise that is idling in the warehouse. They believe that if you have a good price then those warehouses should be moving stocks out fast. The key word is "fast turnover".

Another Chinese doctrine is the word "patience". A businessman should be patient. He should remove the mentality of making a "killing" at the onset. Business is a long time affair. You may make a "killing" on your first salvo but do you think that those same customers will go back to you? When the customer gets burned the first time, you can be sure that you have ended the relationship. Business is built on "relationship". This is our next topic.

THE "SUKI" STRATEGY

The word "suki" (pronounced "soo-kee"), a derivative Chinese word used in the Philippines, means "patron" or a "loyal customer". When they give you this title, you as the customer are given special discounts and extra care and attention. A "suki" gets special treatment. A "suki" is an honor for a Chinese businessman because this customer has proven his loyalty by constantly patronizing his store. Once you hook a customer for being a "suki", that "suki" will never ever buy from another store. You have the customer's loyalty for life. A "suki" has given his outmost loyalty because he has given his full trust in your business. A "suki" knows that you will not put one on him. This term "suki" can also be addressed to the storeowner or businessman himself.

A loyal customer can also address the storeowner as "suki" because they have built this unique relationship over the years. Both of the parties have a debt of gratitude to one another. The businessman is indebted to his customer because of his patronage and the customer is also indebted to the storeowner because of special privileges that the owner extends to him.

If for example, the "suki" is short of cash for the payment of all the merchandise that he purchases, the storeowner will not insist on payment right away. He will just tell the "suki" to just take the merchandise home and just pay whenever he can. That is the trust and confidence that binds the customer and the businessman.

This leads to the next topic regarding trust and the "paperless" contract.

WORD OF HONOR

The "paperless" contract is another Chinese type of doing business. Among the big Chinese businessmen is the practice of "paperless" contracts. One enters into a business transaction or deal without signing any document or legal paper. The business deal is primarily based on trust. Nobody signs anything. The agreement of negotiation may involve millions in terms of monetary value but nobody signs anything. The businessman who extends credit to another businessman in order for him to start his own business does not require the other party to sign anything. It simply means that I fully trust that you are going to repay me back sometime in the future. Or I am extending this credit to you for merchandise you ordered and you do not have to issue me an "i.o.u."

Why is this so? They believe that a paper contract is useless. Even though you may sign a bulk of paperwork or legal documents for an agreement and you really have the intention of deceiving me, then you are definitely going to deceive me. The Chinese businessmen do not want to waste their time in legal battles and court hearings. They simply would not go to that wasteful activity. If you ask him a favor today and he extends it to you, he also expects a similar return of "debt of gratitude" in the future when he goes to you for a very special favor. You are expected to return this favor. That is how it works. There is no need to sign agreements. Your word of honor is highly respected.

THE SECRET BEHIND THE COST OF GOODS

How do the Chinese sell so cheap and still make a profit?

The secret is putting their cost of goods way, way down.

They cut cost on every corner.

They maintain a very simple manufacturing plant. It may not be the state-of-the-art facility as long as it can produce the products at the lowest possible cost. Modernization can wait a while until such time when the businessman can afford it.

I had the privilege of working with big Chinese corporations. I know how they cut costs from the purchase of a box of pencils for office use to ordering more expensive equipments. They will canvass every supplier until they can get the lowest price possible.

Their factories are not a pretty sight to see. Who cares, the factories are not for the public to see anyway. As long as the product looks good when it comes out of the door, that's fine. The customer will never see the difference when he sees the product on the shelf of the grocery or supermarket stores. The Chinese businessmen's main concern is to be able to price his products lower than his competitors.

Manufacturing operations are very simple. They usually hire one factory manager, if possible, whom they pirate from their competitor. They only hire contractual factory workers who they only pay minimum wage and lay them off before their permanency kicks in. They will always try to avoid the provision of the labor law that will make the factory workers a permanent employee a day after their sixth month of employment.

They make it a point to keep their manufacturing cost and their labor costs down as possible. They do not pay benefits because they are only contractual workers except for social security, which the law requires. Then they hire the next batch of factory workers (this is only applicable in countries where there is an oversupply of labor). There is no problem of hiring if it is an employers' market and there is a surplus of laborers.

Inexpensive raw and packaging materials are usually used. The Purchasing department sources the cheapest suppliers. They do not have sophisticated or glamorous offices. They only use second hand office furniture and equipment. Aesthetic aspects are not their primary concern. As long as the workplace is safe then it's fine.

As long as their cost of goods are way below competition then they are confident that can under price and grab market shares from them.

THE IMPORTANCE OF PLACEMENT

A typical Chinese businessman is not very keen on spending millions for mass advertising especially on expensive media such as television. Although they acknowledge the power of television ads, most of them view these as added cost to the product which will add up to the price of the product. They believe that minimal advertising and word of mouth can replace the more expensive form of advertising. They believe that placement is the best alternative to expensive advertising. They believe that their products must be present on the shelves of groceries and supermarkets. That is all they want to accomplish…just place the product on the shelves. They may not be able to afford television ads and they may forgive themselves not to be present on the airwaves. But the sin they won't forgive is when their products are not placed on the shelves.

Why is this so? They firmly believe that once a product is placed on the shelves, it will do the "talking" to the customers moving around the store. They believe in the statistical probability that when the product is on the shelves, the customer in one way or the other will definitely pick it. It may not be picked today but definitely will be picked anytime tomorrow, two days from today, three days from today or next week. But this is what is surely going to happen…it will definitely be picked. If their product is not on the shelves, the battle is lost. By being present on the shelves, you stand a better chance of being sold. That is why they will not take no for an answer if the retailer would not want to stock their products. The retailer cannot say no in reality. If these new products are coming from a regular supplier such as a big corporation like them, the retailers cannot say no. And furthermore, these big retailers are also part of the Chinese syndicate who controls the distribution segment of the industry.

There is no reason to refuse a supplier who belongs to the syndicate. If you are not part of the syndicate and just a newcomer into the arena, then you might have a problem getting into the distribution system. Because having a shelf space in groceries, supermarkets and other outlets is considered POWER. You already have power once your product is displayed on the shelf.

However, not everyone can be given shelf space. Shelf space is very limited and priceless. Most, if not all, of the outlets are already crowded with the same products with only the brand names differentiating them from one another. One additional product, which is basically the same as the other products, is just another annoyance to the retailers How can a new entrant guarantee that the retailer will make money out of his product if it is displayed in the shelf? The retailers would probably accept you provided you give a very good trade discount and free goods. Most of these retailers will only accept stocks from well-established firms.

Instead of spending millions on advertisements, the suppliers give generous "deals" to these retailers. The retailer is given additional discount is he pays earlier than the due date. That is extra money to their pockets. The supplier offers free goods for every number of their products ordered. These are called "product deals".

Many of the retailers of electronics and home appliances in Manila do not really make money on the retail price of the appliances. They price their home appliances at almost dealer cost with very little margin just so they could move out as many appliances as possible. Why? Because the suppliers offer deals on the volume of products sold by the retailer. This is where the retailers make money. They make money because of the deals offered by suppliers. They really do not make much money on the retail price. They know it. That is part of the strategy. They just want to move out as many products as possible out of the door. The more you sell, the more incentives you get from the suppliers. The lower your prices are, the more customers come to you to buy. You develop a reputation as the store that has the lowest price. Your store becomes a bargain center. Customers flock to you because you offer the best price compared with other retailers. Then you become successful.

THE "BUENA MANO" BELIEF

"Buena mano" (pronounced "bwe-nah mah-noh) is a derivative Spanish word. This simply means, "the first sale you make will bring good luck for the rest of the day". This belief is strongly adhered to by Philippine-Chinese retailers. Retailers have this belief that the very first customer that steps inside the store will decide if the day will be great or disastrous in terms sales. They believe that in order for you to be lucky that day and hit your day's sales quota is to give the most generous discount or favor to the first customer who steps inside your store to buy. It is almost mandatory for you to close that first sale in order to break the "spell".

The very first customer seems to be the "lucky charm" that will act as the "ignition" to fire up your engine of sales. This first customer is usually given the utmost in service and favor. This belief is somewhat unbelievable but most Filipino retailers swear that it works all the time.

"FENG SHUI"

Another belief of Chinese businessmen pertains to "feng shui" (pronounced "fong soy"). The literal meaning of the two words is "wind" and "water". Feng shui, in a broad perspective, is a systematic way of how life and things are properly arranged to conform to a universal law. The Chinese says that if you are not aware of the laws of feng shui, then you may be treading on dangerous ground, which may be detrimental either to your business or your way of life.

An example of the principles of feng shui would be the choice of location for your business or how the design of your building should be. These two choices should adhere to the laws and principles of feng shui. Conformance or non-conformance to the laws of feng shui may spell the difference between the success and failure of a business enterprise. Knowledgeable Chinese businessmen would ordinarily hire a feng shui expert before they would choose a location for a business. A feng shui expert will tell you right on the spot whether your location is ideal for business or not. A blueprint of your building design and layout, whether internal or external, will tell the feng shui expert if it will be a structure that would be a blessing to you or a curse. It is said that the design of the ill-fated twin towers building of the World Trade Center in New York does not conform to the feng shui principles. That it is a building doomed from its conception.

Another example of a violation of the feng shui principle was what happened with United Laboratories, Inc. There was an incident that almost drove the company to be unionized. As we discussed earlier in this book, formation of a labor union is a big "no" to the owners of the company. The labor union organizers almost won the battle to have the company unionized in the year 1986. It was the first time in 30 years of the company's existence that it experienced work stoppage and picket lines. Management had the biggest headache of their lives during those turbulent times when the union organizers were trying to formalize the formation of a labor union within the company. After months of grueling legal battle and management's counter offensive against the formation of the labor union, management finally adhered to the conduct of an election to vote for or against the formation of the labor union. But before the election was done, management has already made strategic moves to ensure that the result of the election would be to their favor. But that is another story. When the final ballot was counted, the result came out that the employees unanimously voted against the formation of a labor union.

Because of the trauma that management encountered during the months of turmoil inside the company, Jose Y. Campos, the founder, took a hard look at what factor could have gone wrong. Everything seems to be right. The fringe benefits for employees were one of the best in the industry and other aspects of proper management were in place. The company was professionally managed and no other company was as benevolent as Unilab.

It's been said that after so much soul searching, the owners decided to hire a feng shui expert. The feng shui consultant discovered that the internal halls and corridors of the company building run through the external doors. This is bad according to the principles of feng shui because the wind that comes from the outside doors goes direct inside the building and that same wind bounces off direct to the walls, which signifies "confusion". There is no element that blocks the wind that blows directly inside. It was therefore ordered by the owners to have the corridors realigned to conform to the principles of feng shui. A major renovation was undergone to implement the new facelift in all the buildings of the company. Corridors and halls were redesigned so that they would not be directly facing the doors. You will also notice that the wooden walls of the corporate buildings are engraved with the initials JYC, which means Jose Y. Campos. These engravings are supposed to bring good luck to the company.

With the renovation in place, Mr. Campos believed that the bad spell that plagued the company during the labor problem is now gone and laid to rest.

GOOD LUCK CHILD

The Chinese also believe that if a family has an autistic, a mentally retarded, a mongoloid, or a mentally disabled child, your family will be favored by God and will bless your family with abundant financial fortunes.

You will notice that some of the very wealthy families, whether Chinese or not, have a mentally disabled child and this child seems to act as a "medium" to their financial fortunes. That is why these families take special care of their mentally disabled child because they believe that this child is the one bringing in the good fortune to the family. The child seems to be the good luck charm to the family. God compensates misfortune into another blessing usually in the form of abundant wealth. If the family is involved in business, the business is sure to prosper and grow. There is nothing that can stop the family business from succeeding. The more you care for your abnormal child, the more blessings will come your way.

DON'T INNOVATE, JUST IMITATE

There is a story, or a joke maybe, about why John Gokongwei, a business tycoon in the Philippines, is so successful as a businessman. It is said that when John was still small, he asked his father for the secret of success in business. And his father said "Son, to be successful in business...don't innovate, just imitate". And that is how he did it. John practically copied all the products of San Miguel Corporation, the leading food conglomerate in the Philippines.

This is the same principle that most Asian businessman follow to get ahead of the business game. Because doing research and development takes some time and entails a substantial amount of investment, it is best to copy or imitate first.

This is what the Japanese did after the Second World War. Japan was heavily devastated after the war. To rapidly get up as fast as they can, they have no choice but to copy western or American products to get fast into the ballgame. It was during the 1950's that anything made in Japan was considered "shoddy" or of poor quality. They started doing business by copying. Although they started with poorly crafted products that suffered in terms of quality versus the western products, later on they decided to improve the quality of their products in order to gain credibility and compete on a long-term basis. They started by copying and look at the Japanese products now. They are even ahead of the companies that they copied from.

That is why you will notice that there are a lot of fake or bootleg products of well-known brands such as Levi's, Gucci, Liz Claiborne, Pierre Cardin, Guess, Ralph Lauren and a lot more brands which you can buy cheaper, of course, in any Asian country compared with the original. And there are a lot more when it comes to other product categories. They are copied because they are well known and people buy them even though they know they are copycats because of its lower price. This is a major headache of these legitimate companies because copyright and patent laws are so loose in some Asian countries that anybody can just copy anything. Presently, there is a crackdown on manufacturers of bootleg products.

This business mentality of "copying" or "imitating" in order to get ahead in business is still around. When Japan finally got out of copying or imitating and became a market leader in practically everything from cameras, electronics, appliances, shipbuilding, steel making, and computers and establishing themselves as a country where quality products are made, you will notice that Korea and Taiwan are now doing the same formula which the Japanese did before. Most of the countries in the Southeast Asian region are copying world-renowned products and exporting them at the lower prices.

A STEP-BY-STEP METHOD OF BUILDING AN EMPIRE

John Gokongwei, one of the biggest "taipans"(business moguls or tycoons) in the Philippines, started business literally from scratch. A story is told that he started his business venture by peddling corn in his native province in Cebu (an island in the Visayan region in the Philippines). Corn is one of nature's crops where he got his breaks in business. He was involved in milling and trading corn from which all his succeeding businesses evolved. He became an expert in trading corn that is why he decided to go into other businesses that has something to do with corn. Thereafter, he went into the production of animal feeds since the basic ingredient of course is corn. His company, Universal Robina Feeds is one of the biggest companies milling and distributing animal feeds. His profits from this venture are similar to selling lemonade drink in a garage. His large customers are big commercial farm owners who are growing livestock.

After he has established the feeds business, he then went into chicken broiler and egg layer livestock raising. He built huge chicken farms to grow broiler chicken. After which he built a chicken dressing plant to produce frozen chicken meat to be sold in supermarkets, groceries and wet markets.

Thereafter, he built chicken layer farms to produce eggs. John was able to get the franchise to raise and sell chicken breeds coming from the United States namely Hyline breeders and Starcross breeders. Since he got the exclusive franchise to raise these breeds, he then decided to sell the day-old chicks to the big farm owners of layers and broilers. He then created a sales division that would take care of the sales of day-old chicks to the livestock farm owners. While he was at it, he asked himself why not put up a business of veterinary drugs to take care of the health requirements of the poultry raisers. Thus he created a veterinary company, Robichem pharmaceuticals, to produce and market locally made veterinary drugs. He pirated the chemist working for Johnson and Johnson and made him the production manager.

Since he has already established himself in the poultry business by getting the franchise of those two big American breeding companies, he then decided to go into the swine raising business. John thereafter put up a big hog-raising farm to breed and sell parent stocks to big hog raising farm owners. He got the franchise of the biggest European swine breeder, Seghers, based in Belgium, thereafter, he was granted the license to breed grandparent stocks. Now, John's company, Robina Farms, supplies the meat requirements of some of the biggest canned meat manufacturing companies like Monterey Farms, aside of course for supplying the livestock requirements of the other local breeders.

And since John's poultry farms count as one of the biggest farms in the entire country, these chicken farms produce tons and tons of chicken droppings or manure everyday. And because he is a business-man in a true sense of the word, he did not throw this manure away. He made use of these chicken droppings into a money making machine. He gathered all these droppings and converted them into fer-tilizers. He then put up a factory exclusively for the conversion of these chicken droppings into fertilizer. He set up machines and bagged these fertilizers to be sold to vegetable farmers who found these fertilizers from chicken manure as the best fertilizer to make vegetables grow so healthy. He named his fertilizer brand as Golden Harvest Fertilizers.

And since John has established himself as a magnate in corn and it's by products, he thought of why not make cereal food products and corn chips snacks out of corn. Thus, "Jack and Jill" corn snack was born. John copied the products of Frito Lay and Kellogg's cereals. It was rumored that he even pirated the technical production consultant of Kellogg's corn flakes. John's corn snacks are one of his biggest mon-eymakers. But that's not the end of the story.

After his success in a grain called corn, he went into the manufacturing and marketing of ice cream, noodle soup, canned foods, candies, spaghetti, macaroni and other grocery foodstuffs. He called this food division, the Consolidated Foods Corporation (CFC). His company grew so big that he called his holding company, Robinson Group of Companies. Since he will need financing for his other business endeavors, he decided to go into banking and bought the majority stock of Philippine Commercial and Industrial Bank (PCIB).

He also went into the sugar business by buying one of the biggest sugar milling companies in the Philippines.

He then went to real estate investments by creating the Robinson Land Company.

He went into joint venture with Ramada Hotels and put up the Manila Midtown Ramada Hotel.

Then he went into building mega shopping malls by putting up the Robinson Shopping Malls situated in big urban cities.

Since his only daughter, Robina, took up journalism and wanted to put up her own publication, John bought one of the biggest newspapers in the Philippines, the well-renowned Manila Times. It is like buying the New York Times for your daughter so she can have a job.

He's got so much money that he was able to buy substantial stocks from his major competitor, San Miguel Corporation (SMC), and even became one of its boards of directors. San Miguel found it too late that one of their directors was directly competing with their products. The board tried to boot out John from the board because of conflict of interest. SMC is still trying to boot him out and John is still fighting the board for his retention as a board member.

How was John able to manage such a conglomerate? He put all his brothers to manage each group of company. He has three brothers, namely, James, Johnson, and Henry. Since his father died, John being the eldest son, took the major responsibility of supporting the Gokongwei family. And it was his mother who kept the family and the business going and free from family squabbles. John was the recognized leader of the conglomerate, not only because he is the eldest son but also because he founded these companies and has a keen sense for business. Their real family name is Go. But he renamed his family name by adding the words "kong wei" which mean "shining star" in Chinese. That is why his name now is John Gokongwei. His other brothers still kept the family name Go. When John changed his family name, extraordinary luck came his way. Everything he touches turn to gold.

That is why some of the prominent celebrities in the Philippines changed the spelling of their names because of the belief that mother luck would change their fortune. Now you will see names such as a famous newspaper columnist like Julie Yap-Daza who changed the spelling of her name to Jhulee Yap-Daza. (By adding the letter "H" she believes that it will bring her more luck). Ben Cervantes, a well-known movie director and screenwriter, changed also the spelling of his name to Behn Cervantes. A well-known stage and TV actress-singer by the name of Maya Valdez changed her name to Mitch Valdez and is now getting more contracts for movie and television spots. By changing the spelling of their name, a certain kind of luck came their way. If you think that your name somehow does not give you the luck that you aspire, maybe it is time to change it. Maybe you cannot get a job in a hospital as a doctor because your family name is Sepulcher (no offense meant to all Sepulchers). But if you change your name to Dr. Kristian Barnard, don't you think you can get more patients?

Going back to John, although his brothers may not be gifted as he is, his brothers has really helped him managed the diversified nature of his business. Without the trust and confidence that he has on his brothers, John would find it difficult to manage his business empire. John's style of management is typical of any Chinese. Cut costs on all fronts so he could sell his products cheaper than his competitors thereby getting more volume of sales. He did become successful in cutting costs on every corner, from administrative expenses through manufacturing costs. And his prices were very competitive. Every purchase requisition is carefully scrutinized. Every request for the purchase of a simple box of pencils has to get the approval of one of the brothers. The brothers frown upon entertainment expense by their marketing managers. Since there are some managers who usually abuse entertainment and representation, this is one expense item that has never been approved by management.

OVERLOOKING THE WELFARE OF YOUR WORKERS

There is one expense item that he did not foresee that would later cause him a lot of headaches and this is the salary of his thousands of his employees. He was known to be stingy when it comes to employee pays and benefits. Little did he know that the gripes of his employees turned against him through the power of the labor union that penetrated all his business enterprises.

From then on, almost all of his companies suffered labor strikes that crippled the normal operations of his business and brought losses to him.

Every time that there is a stalemate during the collective bargaining agreement between management and labor, strikes would ignite automatically. This is a common scenario in all of his companies. If your workers feel that you, the owner, do not care about their welfare, the workers will have the same feeling toward you. As the saying goes "the feeling is mutual".

Almost all of his managers are either his relatives, or relatives of his long time managers, friends of managers, friends of his family, friends of friends and so on. Like Jose Y. Campos of Unilab, John Gokongwei does not hire just anybody to manage delicate positions. He, however, considers those who have proven their loyalty towards the company after working for many years. The Chinese businessman or owner does not simply put their trust on anybody unless they have worked for them for most of their lifetime. Trust, confidence and honesty should be earned.

TRAIN YOUR CHILDREN AT AN EARLY AGE

What is so admirable about the Gokongwei's, and most of the Chinese businessmen for that matter, is that they train their children about their business at an early age.

John Gokongwei and his brothers could just provide their children with luxuries and not exposed them to the hardships of putting up and running a business as what other businessmen fathers do. Not with the Gokongwei's. Their children do not enjoy the luxuries of life. They must work hard for it. The children are not pampered with the good things.

John's eldest son, Lance, in his teens worked in the warehouse of his father's company earning minimum wage and eating with the rest of the warehouse workers. Bobby, the son of Johnson Go, also in his teens worked in the ice cream factory as a laborer and was earning minimum wage too just like the other factory workers. They were not given special privileges. They are constantly transferred from one work area to another to get exposed. They do odd jobs in the manufacturing, maintenance, general services, messenger services, clerical, warehousing so they can have an idea of how the company operates from the grassroots level. So when their time comes to take over their father's business, they are well prepared and equipped. They have a better understanding of how the business operates and have better judgments later on when they take over the overall management of the firm.

Many of the Chinese businessmen teach their children to mend the store. These kids do retail sales, warehousing, and restocking on the display shelves.

They are not like the typical teen-ager who just lofts around the house playing video games, partying or doing drugs. They are not parasites in the family. They do not ask for money or allowance. They work hard to earn their keep. A typical Chinese family instills the value of money among their children. No matter how the parents can afford to give them the luxuries of life, the children have to work for the money that they receive. There is no dole out here. There is no free ride. Every penny counts. A missing penny out of your 99 cents will not make a dollar.

They are better prepared to go into business. Early training in business and discipline in handling money are the keys to their success. They are taught to value nickels and dimes because of the small profit they add on to the price of their merchandise.

0-595-22723-6

www.ingramcontent.com/pod-product-compliance
Lightning Source LLC
Chambersburg PA
CBHW030805180526
45163CB00003B/1152